Endorsements

I wish I had this stuff earlier! Easy ideas and tools that make family time more meaningful. Small Moments = Huge Impact. The reminder to be present is priceless. Watching other parents make real, intentional connections with their kids is inspiring, game-changing value creation!

—Melanie Daughtery, Arizona

It's a space where parenting doesn't feel lonely; other families get it. The tools we've learned have helped bring peace and consistency into our home. They've given our family language for things we struggled to explain, such as confidence and contribution.

—Heather Boone, Pennsylvania

I like having a real, tangible way to teach my kids about money and prepare them for adulthood. The tools and handouts make it all feel simple and actually doable. I love being around parents who want to raise confident kids, too, families who are just as intentional about growing future leaders.

—Kasey Ryan, Texas

This community reminds me that I'm not alone; there's always someone who gets what I'm going through as a parent. It's a space where I can be honest about the hard stuff and celebrate the small wins without judgment. Everything aligns with one framework, so I'm not guessing what to try next.

—Heather Peterson, Colorado

Dinner Table® has helped us tune out all the outside noise about what our kids "should" be doing and instead focus on what they're actually capable of. I found this amazing community of parents who believe that our kids can do so much more than society gives them credit for. It's not just about money or financial lessons; it's about raising great humans to contribute to our family, community, and the world. Dinner Table teaches real-life skills while building character, empathy, and resilience. My child is learning to be aware of her emotions, to think of others, and to see mistakes as part of the process, not something to be afraid of. I love that Dinner Table isn't just focused on financial success, but on helping kids grow into capable, kind, and confident adults. Dinner Table has truly changed the way I parent and the way my daughter sees herself in our family.

—Addie Aman, Oklahoma

We are happy for the change we have seen in our children. This has given purpose to how we raise our children. Now our children are looking for ways to help around the household. Thank you!

—The Taylor Family, Arizona

Before Dinner Table, getting my kids involved in chores was a battle. Now they see it as teamwork, and our evenings are so much calmer.

—The Martin Family, Arizona

My favorite part of the community/resources is that they really care. Lee, Michael, Kasey, and the rest of the team are supportive and want to help families. I love how they are all about the community and pouring into the community consistently. It is very inspiring and a reminder of the good people in the world!

—Andre Abrams, Arizona

I have a 13-year-old son. In school, he was just passed along without truly learning what he needed to know to be successful in life. Thank you so very much.

—The Phillips Family, Arizona

VALUE CREATION FAMILY

THE PROVEN PLAYBOOK FOR SETTING UP YOUR FAMILY TO ENJOY TRUE SUCCESS

VALUE CREATION FAMILY

THE PROVEN PLAYBOOK FOR SETTING UP YOUR FAMILY TO ENJOY TRUE SUCCESS

Lee Benson

ethos
collective

VALUE CREATION FAMILY © 2026 by Lee Benson. All rights reserved.

Printed in the United States of America

Published by Igniting Souls
PO Box 43, Powell, OH 43065
IgnitingSouls.com

This book contains material protected under international and federal copyright laws and treaties. Any unauthorized reprint or use of this material is prohibited. No part of this book may be reproduced or transmitted in any form or by any means, electronic or mechanical, including photocopying, recording, or by any information storage and retrieval system, without express written permission from the author.

LCCN: 2025927454
Paperback ISBN: 978-1-63680-597-9
Hardcover ISBN: 978-1-63680-598-6
e-Book ISBN: 978-1-63680-599-3

Available in paperback, hardcover, e-book, and audiobook.

Any Internet addresses (websites, blogs, etc.) and telephone numbers printed in this book are offered as a resource. They are not intended in any way to be or imply an endorsement by Igniting Souls, nor does Igniting Souls vouch for the content of these sites and numbers for the life of this book.

Some names and identifying details may have been changed to protect the privacy of individuals.

The content of this book reflects the author's personal experiences, opinions, and interpretations. The inclusion of any individual, living or deceased, or any organization or entity, is not intended to malign, defame, or harm the reputation of such persons or entities. All statements regarding individuals are solely the author's perspective and do not represent verified facts unless expressly cited to a verifiable source.

The publisher has not independently investigated or confirmed the accuracy of any such references and disclaims all responsibility for them. Nothing in this book should be construed as factual assertions about the character, conduct, or reputation of any individual or entity mentioned. Any resemblance to persons living or dead is purely coincidental unless explicitly stated.

The publisher expressly disclaims liability for any alleged loss, damage, or injury arising from any perceived defamatory content or reliance upon statements within this work. Responsibility for the views, depictions, and representations rests solely with the author.

The superscript symbol IP listed throughout this book is known as the unique certification mark created and owned by Instant IP^{IP}. Its use signifies that the corresponding expression (words, phrases, chart, graph, etc.) has been protected by Instant IP^{IP} via smart contract. Instant IP^{IP} is designed with the patented smart contract solution (US Patent: 11,928,748), which creates an immutable time-stamped first layer and fast layer identifying the moment in time an idea is filed on the blockchain. This solution can be used in defending intellectual property protection. Infringing upon the respective intellectual property, i.e., IP, is subject to and punishable in a court of law.

DEDICATION

To the next generation of value creators.
Kids today will be running the world of tomorrow,
and I want it to be amazing!

TABLE OF CONTENTS

Foreword 15

A Few More Thoughts from a Parent 17

Note to the Reader: Why This Matters 21

Chapter 1: Start with Adulthood in Mind 29
    The Best Time to Begin Is Today

Chapter 2: Establish a Value Creation Family 42
    We Have the Power to Create Material,
    Emotional, and Spiritual Value

**Chapter 3: Creating House Rules Leads
to Better Relationships** 56
    Households Run Better When Everyone
    Is Doing What Is Expected of Them

Chapter 4: Build Your Kids' Financial Competency 67
    Create an Environment Where Your Kids
    Understand Money

**Chapter 5: Turn Struggle Into Strength
for Your Family** 90
    Every Obstacle Contains an Opportunity

Chapter 6: Don't Settle for Going Solo 104
    Tap into Deeper Family Wisdom

Chapter 7: Lead Clearly and Boldly. 116
    Every Family Member Has an Influential Role

Appendix: Getting Started 139
Bibliography. 153
Acknowledgments. 155
About the Author 157

FOREWORD

I first met Lee Benson through two passionate mothers who had created a financial literacy app for kids. During our conversation, Lee mentioned his company, Dinner Table, which helps families and children thrive. At the time, I didn't think much of it until my husband's curiosity about Lee's music led us to visit him. That visit changed everything. Sitting in Lee's home, I learned about his extraordinary life—a journey marked by struggles, resilience, and remarkable accomplishments, and the powerful concept behind Dinner Table.

Curious to see it in action, I accepted Lee's invitation to attend one of his monthly facilitated discussions with a community of low- to moderate-income families. Walking in, I wondered: How will he connect with people who seem so different from him? What I witnessed was inspiring. Lee led conversations about value creation, healthy and unhealthy struggles, and personal growth. There were laughs, tears, and heartfelt stories shared across families. The connection was undeniable: no fear, no judgment, only determination and a shared desire to learn and thrive.

As president and CEO of a nonprofit serving hundreds of thousands of students with financial, economic, and entrepreneurial skills, I thought to myself: *This is powerful. More students need to experience this.* After inviting Lee to speak at a local high school, the feedback was immediate and enthusiastic.

Students echoed his message: "You can start anywhere and go everywhere."

Lee and I share one thing in common: we both left home at the age of seventeen. My reasons were very different, but I cannot imagine the adversities Lee faced, both intentional and unintentional, and the strength it took to overcome them and become CEO of several successful companies.

Dinner Table was born from Lee's personal struggles and hard-earned wisdom. It offers lessons that benefit families, workplaces, and communities alike. With my background in economics and finance, I see Dinner Table as a living example of economic principles in action. It teaches families to create productive family systems with goals, roles, incentives, choices, and consequences, empowering every member of a household. It embodies the economic principle of trade and voluntary exchange, which creates wealth, and most importantly, value creation—the foundation of prosperity for nations, communities, families, and individuals.

What I love most is how Dinner Table brings families together like a team sport. It helps parents and children build values, embrace and leverage struggles, and develop resilience to create lasting legacies. While financial literacy is part of the program, Dinner Table goes beyond wealth creation. It connects financial literacy to the broader goal of creating value in life.

I hope this book inspires and motivates you as much as it did me.

—Elena Zee
President and CEO
Arizona Council on Economic Education

A FEW MORE THOUGHTS FROM A PARENT

"You need to understand the value of a dollar."

My dad would say this to me until he was blue in the face, and I would turn red in the face hearing it every time I asked for a few unearned dollars. How unfair life is to a pre-teen with no job or money. When I got my first job at the local pizza joint at sixteen, I finally understood what he was saying, becoming conscious of the money going out and coming in, and how it was determined by what I valued.

I remember a friend of mine buying a brand-new 110 CC dirt bike when we were about seventeen.

"How'd you afford this?" I asked.

"You can finance it."

After he explained what that meant, the idea of putting a small amount of money down, splitting it into payments, and getting a dirt rocket that my friends and I could illegally ride through suburban neighborhoods seemed very appealing. I mean, what do you value at that age? I valued time with my friends and the infinite possibilities of mischief to add to my collection of short, youthful years.

My friend forgot the part where those payments included interest, which my dad talked about with great disdain regarding credit cards. But this wasn't a credit card; it was a loan. This was the day I learned a new phrase from my father: "If you don't have the cash for a want, then you can't afford it." Oh yes, the wants vs. needs conversation. Those two things were very muddied and intertwined in my teenage brain. I needed food, but was still living with my dad. I needed a place to live, and I had that, so I also needed the dirt bike? I didn't get the dirt bike.

The next year, I started understanding the "needs" conversation more as I was removed from my dad's car insurance, medical insurance and introduced to discussions on the price of college. Being an adult gets expensive fast, and what you value becomes what you spend your money on. If you value money and understand the value of having it, you'll invest, you'll live below your means, you'll save for those wants, and you'll understand the phrase your dad said until you stopped hearing it and began living it.

I'm forty years old now. I have an amazing wife of thirteen years and two children, a daughter, nine, and a son, six. Despite the tumultuous road I created for myself in my twenties, I always came back to the lessons my dad taught me, even when I didn't want to receive them. Despite my mistakes, I always had this work ethic, this grit, this voice that fought against my character flaws and ego-driven trivialities. I made some bad financial decisions—gambling, drug usage, and unnecessary spending—but I stayed away from credit card debt, loans (drug dealer loans don't count), and the kind of money habits that are hard to come back from. I walked a thin line between being detrimentally irresponsible and responsible enough not to ruin my life forever.

Then I met my wife, who left home at eighteen, went to hair school, and became self-employed, which she still is today. Her financial literacy and responsibility far surpassed mine. Like most married couples in their late twenties, we started out broke, got smashed with taxes our first year, but held on to what we knew to be true: the value of a dollar. We saved, we struggled, we built businesses, we invested, and we bought our first home together.

In this home, we welcomed our two children, and what we valued in life became clearer every day after that. In this home, we began raising our children on the foundation we created. In this home, we changed with the seasons of life, grew with them, and taught them what a good human being is, not by telling, but by showing.

As a dad now, I have a phrase I haven't told my children yet, but every day I hope they feel it. It goes: "Whatever is going on in the world, whatever outside influences there are, it doesn't matter because what is taught, shown, answered, and connected through happens between these four walls."

That's why I'm excited for families to read Value Creation Family, it reinforces the same lessons many of us learned the hard way and offers a clearer path for passing them on to our kids.

In this home.

Jon Gustin
Creator, @thetireddad
Author, *The Tired Dad: 100 Reflections on Showing Up for What Matters Most*

NOTE TO THE READER: WHY THIS MATTERS

What do you want for your family? Tough question.

It's easy to worry about the future. If you're like most people, you know outside influences are trying to sabotage your kid's ability to create value in the world. If we're honest, it's difficult to serve as a model. We have our own battles 24/7. It's difficult for family members to be united as a team, much less create value in the world. Don't despair. You're not alone. And in this book, you'll find tremendous hope as you unpack a simple success model.

For me, it all started about ten years ago when I got involved with an Arizona-based nonprofit focused on improving conditions for K-12 students to learn: *A For Arizona*.

I helped operate the nonprofit, served on the Board of Directors, coached their CEO, and donated over a million dollars of my own money to their cause. In total, we raised over one hundred million dollars and poured it into innovation in education, transportation, and other programs to improve conditions for K-12 students to learn. Why? Simple. Because our kids are truly our future, and this fact will impact all of us.

Unfortunately, every time our team went to the State Legislature, all the adults fought over money; it was never about the kids. This got me thinking more deeply about two things: what is the purpose of an education, and how can we solve this problem in a way that works at scale?

First, the purpose. The purpose of an education is to create value in the world. Period. The current system encourages kids to get good grades, a diploma, a degree, and then a job. There's nothing inspiring about the current system. No wonder kids aren't motivated. No wonder they check out emotionally. And no wonder education is often referred to as a *conveyor-belt system*.

Repeatedly, I hear that if kids have access to an education, it will ensure their success in life. This simply isn't true across the board. A better way to frame this would be: Giving kids access to the right education, based on the value they want to create in the world, will set them up for success.

The right education that supports the value each kid wants to create in the world is the way forward. Why isn't our education system framing it this way? After all, it seems so obvious. The primary reason literacy scores for kids have been declining (on average) for decades is because we haven't been connecting the dots from education to creating value in the world. We've been pouring more money into a broken system, but that isn't improving anything.

I believe this so much, I even had T-shirts made up that say, *Money and Memorization Is Not Education, Learning to Create Value in the World Is Education*.

Now, how to address the problem at scale? It hit me early in my time with A For Arizona that it would be almost impossible to fix this from inside the current education system. We needed to approach the problem from outside the system by building a community of parents raising kids who create value in the world. Families should own their kids' education, not an outside system filled with conflicts of interest.

VALUE CREATION FAMILY

Building a community of parents with the mission of raising kids who create value in the world will move the needle. It always has. The idea is simple, but not always easy to do. When parents get involved in every aspect of their kids' education, their kids' worlds change. Then *their* world changes, and finally, *the* world can change! First, by identifying, exploring, and refining how their kids want to create value in the world now and when they launch into adulthood. And also by being a driving force in education reform, so the education system moves toward fully supporting the true purpose of an education for its customers, our kids.

Fast forward to today, I took over in May 2025 as CEO of a failed kids banking app company and reset the business to build a community of parents raising kids that create value in the world. In the first year (as of the writing of this book), we have over forty thousand parents in our community from sixty-seven countries. In the next three to four years, we can grow that number to millions. We changed the name of the company and now call it Dinner Table® Family.

My vision has evolved from focusing solely on the kids to creating holistic value as a family. That said, the foundation for every family's future is the kids. This book is focused on helping parents raise kids who create value in the world, and how every family member contributes to creating value as a family.

When it comes to what kids are capable of, many self-limiting beliefs exist. This applies to adults, too, for that matter. I work with dozens of families, and it is fulfilling for me to watch the culture shift from concern about the future to one of hope. I love hearing kids realize and proclaim, "I can create value!" One of the best parts of being in this community is seeing them shed those self-limiting beliefs that held them back way too long.

This is true regardless of income levels. I believe the largest untapped value creation potential lies in kids from lower-income households because they have the drive to want more. This is because they typically struggle more. The challenge is unlocking this potential by changing their beliefs about what's possible. I know because this is where I started.

I grew up in a low-income family where there were many negative emotions and behaviors associated with money. My early home environment wasn't the healthiest, with some family members in and out of prison over the years. My parents kicked me out of the house at the beginning of my senior year in high school, saying it was because I was never home due to my work and school schedule. But I knew it was from growing conflict over a values misalignment between my parents and me. By then, I was financially competent and independent with zero family support financially. Most kids today aren't financially competent and fully financially self-reliant until well after the age of eighteen.

So what made me different?

I grew up in what felt like two worlds. One was my family environment, which was culturally in conflict with how I wanted to show up in the world. The other was the outside world, where I would work for neighbors and companies not associated with my family or friends to earn money. This started when a neighbor, unsolicited, asked me to pull weeds in her garden for twenty-five cents an hour. Back then, that was a lot of money for a six-year-old, and I remember the energy that shot throughout my body when I finished and got paid. I had a sense of pride, and it felt amazing!

From pulling weeds, I moved up to shoveling snow, mowing lawns, paper routes, odd jobs, dishwasher, busboy, and finally cooking at a restaurant at the time I was kicked out of the house. I spent the first night in the truck I had purchased with my own money, and the second night I moved into an apartment with a roommate. Being kicked out was one of the best things that ever happened to me.

I call what I went through the Value-Creation-Cycle. I would struggle to develop a capability, which built my confidence. I would then use that capability to create value and get paid for it. As I learned to create more and more value by increasing my capability, I would get paid more. See Figure 1 below.

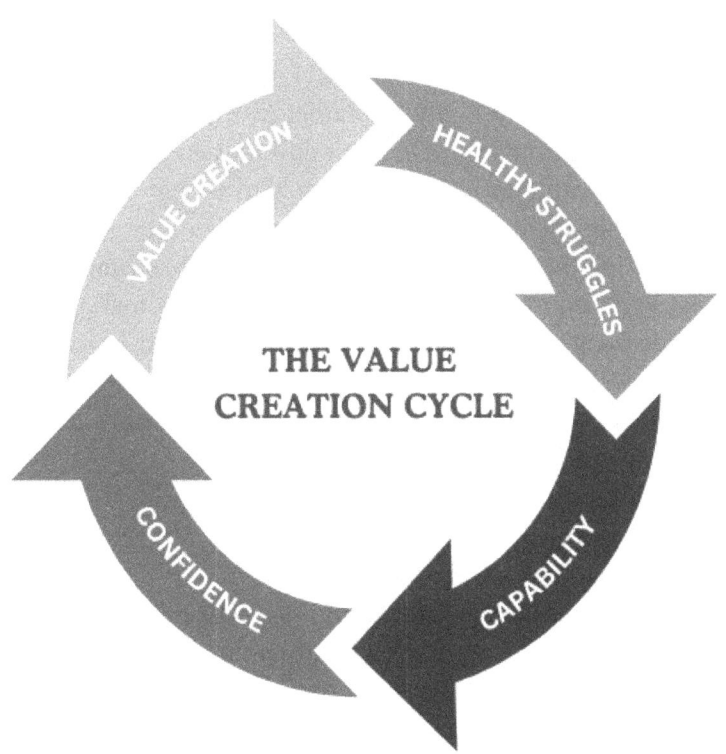

Figure 1. The Value Creation Cycle

Early on, I knew I had to earn more. I was doing well supporting myself through my senior year when my parents put an additional ankle weight on me around the time I graduated. My mom charged up four credit cards in my name because they had my social security number. The balance on each card was over $2,000, with interest rates well over 20 percent. She advised me to file for bankruptcy, and all would be fine. I wasn't the only sibling they did this to. I chose to pay them off over time so I wouldn't have a bankruptcy on my record. And I chose not to report them so they wouldn't go to jail. It took years to get out from under this debt; I was earning six dollars an hour at the time.

A note regarding my parents. I never knew my natural father and thought of my stepfather as my dad. My parents made many mistakes that I won't go into here. By the time I was on my own, I realized they had a hard enough time getting through life themselves, let alone raising five kids. I actually felt bad for them that they struggled with life so much, but there was nothing I could do. They were adults making their own decisions. They have both since passed, and I wish they could have approached life with more value creation in mind. Reflecting on my early experiences, I wouldn't change a thing. In most cases, being the opposite of how my parents showed up taught me how I wanted to show up in life regarding my character and beliefs. Even in an unhealthy struggle, there is value to be found, and I am forever grateful.

Now I practice the value creation cycle, and taking bigger steps each time, I have started eight companies from scratch. As of the writing of this book, I have sold three of them, one for well into nine figures. The point is that you can start from *anywhere* and go *everywhere*. I came from a low-income family with debt as my only graduation present, and I was still able to create multi-generational wealth from zero.

I've learned that value creation is so much more than just financial gain. When I figured this out, it actually led to me earning a lot more money. Approaching value creation holistically—material, emotional, and spiritual value—supercharges everything you do. My goal with this book is to help you intentionally create value as a family and launch your kids into adulthood as amazing, value-creating adults!

Chapter 1

START WITH ADULTHOOD IN MIND

The Best Time to Begin Is Today

When your kids launch into adulthood at eighteen years old, what will that look like? How much thought have you put into it? Are you aware of how your kids want to show up as adults?

We titled this chapter "Start with Adulthood in Mind," a little twist on the now-famous quote by Steven Covey. In his international bestseller, *The 7 Habits of Highly Effective People*, he encourages his readers to define future outcomes, so they can shape present actions. This purpose filters, then influences everything we think and do. Similarly, if we start with who we want our kids to be as adults, we can adjust current parenting to arrive at that intended destination.

Often, when I talk about this concept with parents, depending on the age of their kids, they might be tempted to feel shame and regret, which is not the point of this exercise. For this reason, we chose the chapter subtitle, "The Best Time to Begin Is Today." We can't change the past. However, we *can* shape the future. It's similar to the famous quote, "The best time to plant a tree was twenty years ago. The second-best time is today."

No child experiences transformation if we wallow in regret about not starting a value creation family sooner. Instead, as you read this book, I encourage you to get inspired about what you can do now, rather than focus on what you might have done a few years ago.

One of my favorite stories about someone taking action is about a friend's son who, along with his good friend, started a business hanging Christmas lights while in high school. In their first season, they earned $38,000. Four years later, they have well surpassed $200,000 in a season. Their new goal is to break $300,000 this upcoming season. I know many older adults who would love to earn this much money in a year, and now, these young adults are earning it in four months of hard yet fun work!

A good way to frame the readiness of your kids to become successful adults is in character, beliefs, and capabilities. Identify the character, beliefs, and capabilities that will make your kids the most successful as adults, and then connect the dots to how they will benefit each kid and the family as a whole.

- Character: How you show up.
- Beliefs: What you think is possible.
- Capabilities: What you can do.

Foundationally, it is important for your kids to have a motivated reason to want to work on these three traits. I love starting with the question, "How do you want to create value in the world?" A child's answer changes as they grow closer to adulthood. When they are younger, how they create value revolves around what they are good at, what they are interested in, and how they like to create value for the family. As kids get older, we can start asking the questions about how they would like to create value when they become adults. In chapter 2, we will take a deeper dive into the three different categories of creating value: material, emotional, and spiritual.

> I LOVE STARTING WITH THE QUESTION, "HOW DO YOU WANT TO CREATE VALUE IN THE WORLD?"

CHARACTER

Character is comprised of the qualities that make up an individual's personality. Naturally, character influences their thoughts, feelings, and actions. These qualities can be categorized as positive or negative. Forging character traits within your kids that will make them successful as adults will be easier to do if you model them as a parent.

Establishing a *why* for your kids to intentionally work on developing character is key. One way to start is to ask your kids if they would like more freedom and decision-making autonomy. Most kids would like more of this, even at a very young age. The next question is, "What do you think it will take to earn these privileges?" These questions lead well into having meaningful character discussions with your kids.

One character trait that usually rises to the top of the list for kids wanting to earn more freedom and decision-making autonomy is integrity. The observable form of integrity is doing what you say. This came up during one of the in-person Dinner Table® communities I lead in Phoenix, Arizona. A young girl going into middle school lit up with a big smile and said yes when I asked her if she wanted more freedom and decision-making rights. With her parents sitting next to her, I then asked, "What do you think it will take to earn this?" It went right to always doing what she said she would do. She admitted that she had a difficult time doing that. She understood the value of developing integrity as a character trait because it would manifest, in the future, more of what she wants now. Her parents beamed throughout the entire conversation.

From there, we turned to the topic of the value of all family members doing what they say they will. With all kids owning their jobs for the family, they don't need to be reminded several times to clean their room and other things they agreed to do consistently.

Think about their futures: What about when your kids become adults? How will having strong integrity benefit them then?

I have employed thousands of people over the years in my various companies, and in my experience, only about 20 percent of them did what they said they would over 90 percent of the time. These team members would be given opportunities for advancement and growth before the other 80 percent because we could count on them. Team members with this character trait have strong organizational trust. Having integrity when your kids launch into adulthood gives them a big advantage over the majority of young adults starting their careers.

There are hundreds of character traits to choose from. Only you can know which is best for your kids and family. The challenge is picking the few most important ones that will help your kids now and when they launch into adulthood. Character traits are filters for decision-making; they shape how you show up in the world, and influence how others experience you.

When considering the most valuable character traits, there are three questions to ask:

1. How will the trait benefit you now?
2. How will it benefit the family?
3. How will it benefit your kids when they become adults?

Be sure to always collaborate with your kids so they fully own their character development.

Here are a few character traits to consider:

- Integrity
- Curiosity
- Honesty
- Compassion
- Cooperative
- Creativity
- Present

- Resiliency
- Calm
- Loyalty
- Respectfulness
- Diligence
- Adaptability
- Generosity

- Humility
- Ambition
- Confidence
- Courage
- Persistence
- Fearlessness
- Affectionate

BELIEFS

Beliefs are powerful. In short, they shape possibilities for the value your kids will create in the world. Where do our beliefs come from? What shapes them? It comes down to our cumulative life experiences, especially beliefs conveyed and modeled by those we respect and love. Our kids derive a significant part of their belief structure from their parents. Whatever parents believe is and is not possible is frequently adopted by their kids.

In a recent Dinner Table in-person group of about eighty parents and kids, I facilitated the topic of how your kids will launch into adulthood. A mother shared that she is always telling her kids they can do anything they set their minds to. Yet, at the same time, she always verbalizes negative and limiting beliefs in front of her kids. She finally "got it" and committed to changing how she thinks and talks about herself, especially when her kids are present. If limitless possibilities apply to our kids, why aren't adults applying the same standard of possibilities to themselves?

Over the past ten years, I have spoken to over four thousand high school students about the virtues of entrepreneurship. Most of these events were small groups of twenty to fifty at a time. During these two-hour discussions, I often opened up with two questions.

1. "If you could meet anyone in the world, whom would it be?" The room always lights up with kids shouting out who they would most like to meet. Everyone from sports stars, world leaders, influencers, actors, singers, celebrities, and more.
2. "What do you think your chances of meeting this person are?" The answer is zero to none 99 percent of the time. At the end of these two-hour discussions, the kids' answers to the second question completely changes. I love how quickly these discussions modify kids' limiting beliefs.

During these sessions, I shared with the kids that when I graduated from high school, I wanted to pursue five career paths or start at least five businesses before I retired, so that any one of them would maintain my lifestyle in retirement. At the time, my thinking was that I could fail at four and still be good. Back then, I observed many older adults whose lives had not turned out well financially as they approached or were already in retirement.

VALUE CREATION FAMILY

I did not want that to be true for me when I reached retirement. Also, I wanted to earn a living in one or both of the two areas I was passionate about: *business* and *music*. In the first half of the 1980s, I played guitar in a three-piece rock band that performed over a thousand times at various venues. It's how I made most of my money back then. Although I don't count it as one of the eight businesses I have started so far, it was definitely like running a business. We had a sound and light crew and a gig-booking manager. We changed out the rhythm sections (employees) a few times, did budgeting, navigated cash flow concerns, and more!

There were two people I wanted to meet, one in music and the other in business. On the music side, it was the American guitarist and songwriter Steve Vai. I love listening to and writing instrumental rock songs, and Steve Vai is as good as it gets in how his music speaks to me. I did some research and found that Steve was facilitating a four-day camp for guitar players limited to 150 attendees. I immediately signed up. It was four extraordinary days of learning from Steve Vai and several other amazing guitarists, including Al Di Meola, Zakk Wylde, and many others.

On the evening of day one, Steve asked for one of the attendees to come up and jam with him and his band. All I heard around me was other guitar players saying they weren't going to be first. So, of course, I ran on stage to be the first to jam with Steve. It was an amazing experience, and since then, I have had the honor of playing with Steve and his band on two more occasions.

Here is a case where I wanted to meet someone aligned with my passion, made it happen, and found Steve Vai to be the most impactful guitar instructor I have ever had. Music is still a powerful hobby for me today, and I wrote and recorded an album with an amazing singer and a good friend of mine in 2024. Our band is called LANDED.

The second example I share with the kids is purely business-related. I really admired Jack Welch, chairman and CEO of General Electric from 1981 to 2001. Jack built the most valuable company in the world and was named Manager of the Century by *Fortune Magazine* in 1999. Similar to how I met Steve Vai, I discovered Jack was facilitating a two-and-a-half-day leadership course limited to one hundred attendees. I signed up as fast as I could to secure my place.

During the first day with Jack and ninety-nine other business leaders, it was clear I was running the smallest business represented in the room. Most attendees were managing over a billion dollars in business; my aerospace business was generating around ten million in revenue at the time. The initial exercise that day required someone from each table to talk about their mission and supporting values. My table was called on first, and because I was the only one who knew and lived their mission and values, I was called upon to share. After a long, uncomfortable silence, Jack said that "is perfect," and he wouldn't change a thing. All the other tables followed, and what they presented sounded more like marketing slogans, not fundamental drivers of creating value in an organization.

At lunch, Jack found me sitting at a table and said, "I've done this thousands of times, and no one has gotten it right until you. How the hell did you do it?" My answer was, and still would be today, that although our businesses were drastically different in size, we were solving for the same problem. And furthermore, if we apply math, common sense, facts, logic, and reason to solving for the problem of creating the most value as a company, we will likely travel the same path, discovering the same timeless approaches. Jack and I quickly became friends, and he and his wife, Suzy, joined my company, ETW (Execute to Win), as partners.

One of my primary goals in working with kids is removing limiting beliefs. After going through the two-hour discussion on the virtues of entrepreneurship and telling these stories of meeting two people I admired, I ask the question again, slightly rephrased: "How many of you still believe you won't be able to meet the person in the world you most wanted to meet at the beginning of our time together?" It goes from zero to just about 100 percent every time. Many changed who they wanted to meet after realizing their chances increased significantly when their passions aligned with the famous person they wanted to meet.

Other limiting beliefs many of these high school students have are around their chances of being successful in life when they become adults. Some common ones are:

"My family doesn't have money, so I never will either."

"No one in my family has ever gone to college, so I won't either and will probably never move from this town."

"I would love to start a business someday, but I just don't think that will be possible."

By the end of these robust two-hour discussions, the majority of the kids transition their beliefs from "I probably can't" to "I can start from anywhere and go everywhere." It can be a great exercise with your kids to list beliefs that will help them be successful in life and those that will limit their success. I believe none of us has any idea what's possible regarding what we can accomplish. Only by pushing the limits of how and where we create value in the world can we move in the direction of realizing this and start removing more of our limiting beliefs.

CAPABILITIES

It's a powerful exercise identifying the foundational capabilities that will be most helpful to your kids' success when they launch into adulthood. As a parent, think back to your past. What answer would you have given when you turned eighteen?

When I ask teenagers whether they would rather be dependent on their family or government programs when they become an adult, or be self-reliant, they always say self-reliant. With that in mind, what are the capabilities they will need to start down this road?

When I was kicked out of the house at seventeen, there were many things we take for granted as adults that I had to figure out fast. Even something as simple as where to do my laundry. I no longer had a washer and dryer down the hallway. I believe there is real value in figuring out some of these more minor things on the fly when there is no other good option. What was I going to do, skip doing laundry? In such cases, we learn quickly to establish habits that enable us to be more self-reliant.

A kid figuring out how to do laundry is relatively easy. There are many more significant foundational capabilities our kids need when they become adults. As I reflect on that time, making, managing, and budgeting money was immediately a priority. Fortunately, I had a big advantage because I had already been working for some time. The difference was that my safety net disappeared overnight. I could not afford to lose my job! I knew I had to get even better at making, managing, saving, and budgeting money.

I also learned that communication skills are incredibly important. I learned that asking for what you want at work and communicating with many different personalities was a required skill if I wanted to advance faster. I didn't care much for English as a subject in high school, but once I had to start writing because it was a job requirement, suddenly I had to care! It's amazing how much faster and better we learn when the learning is tied to something we want.

Generally, to be a successful adult, we require mastery in some very important capability categories. These include skills regarding money, communication, relationships, career, identifying and navigating people with hidden agendas, and so on. But what about all the little things? Some other skills I had to figure out quickly in my first year as an adult included:

- Interviewing for a job
- Writing a résumé
- Getting health insurance
- Acquiring automobile insurance on my own
- Getting utilities turned on
- Activating a telephone line
- Opening a bank account
- Getting a credit card
- Finding economical ways to maintain my vehicle
- Grocery shopping on a budget I could afford
- Dealing with people trying to take advantage of me

I could list more, but you get the point. These seemingly smaller things can overwhelm a new adult if they aren't ready for them. And the dilemma is compounded if they lack strong skills related to money, communication, and general life skills.

The earlier you can start, the better when it comes to discussing and developing the capabilities that will help your kids become successful adults. Start small and take bigger and bigger steps at a pace that works for your kids. We will explore this more in the following chapters.

I love having conversations with parents and kids about how they want to launch into adulthood with respect to character, beliefs, and capabilities. And then working backwards to where the kids are currently to put a plan in place to ensure they will be ready when the time comes.

I believe all parents want their kids to be successful as adults. At the same time, a high percentage of kids are not ready to be self-reliant at eighteen. Why is this? Most parents are doing many great things, but often not in an intentional and organized way. To help them, I have developed something called The Dinner Table® Method^{IP}. The Dinner Table Method is made up of four simple things you can implement to intentionally create value as a family:

1. Value Creation
2. House Rules
3. Financial Competency
4. Healthy Struggle

More on these four pillars in the following chapters.

A benefit of having over forty thousand parents in our Dinner Table Family communities is that I see a much broader spectrum of what works and what does not. Most parents are incredibly busy and ask, "How will I find the time to implement something like this in my family?" We are seeing one example after another of where implementing The Dinner Table Method^{IP} is saving time for parents and creating a more energized family culture.

In one community I lead, a single mother of three boys established everyone's job for the family as part of House

Rules. One of the jobs included the boys cooking dinner six nights each week. Now, Mom cooks dinner just one night a week and gets to enjoy meals her sons cook, watching them develop this capability. This is a huge time-saver for Mom and a confidence builder for the boys as they shift to creating value for the family.

In the next four chapters, I will cover the elements of the Dinner Table Method in greater detail.

BIGGEST TAKEAWAYS FROM CHAPTER 1:

- Be intentional and thoughtful about how you want your kids to launch into adulthood.
- Identify the character traits that will represent how your kids will show up in the world, how others experience them, and provide an important filter for making decisions.
- Beliefs drive what is and is not possible.
- Model the beliefs you want to instill within your kids.
- Work with your kids to develop the capabilities that will enable them to be successful, self-reliant adults.
- Implement the Dinner Table Method, a simple and sound way to establish an intentional value-creation culture within your family.

Chapter 2

ESTABLISH A VALUE CREATION FAMILY

We Have the Power to Create Material, Emotional, and Spiritual Value

I have yet to meet a family that doesn't want to strengthen their ability to create value as a family. Establishing such a culture creates an environment for kids that significantly increases their chances of being successful adults. It also increases the family's chances of building on their legacy for multiple generations.

The first pillar of the Dinner Table Method is *Value Creation,* with its three categories of value creation: material value (money), emotional value (energy), and spiritual value (connectedness). The goal is to create value as a family in the right balance between these three categories. Each family member can have a slightly to significantly different balance of the three categories that works best for them. Taking a holistic approach to creating value significantly improves how we feel going through life. Isn't that what really matters?

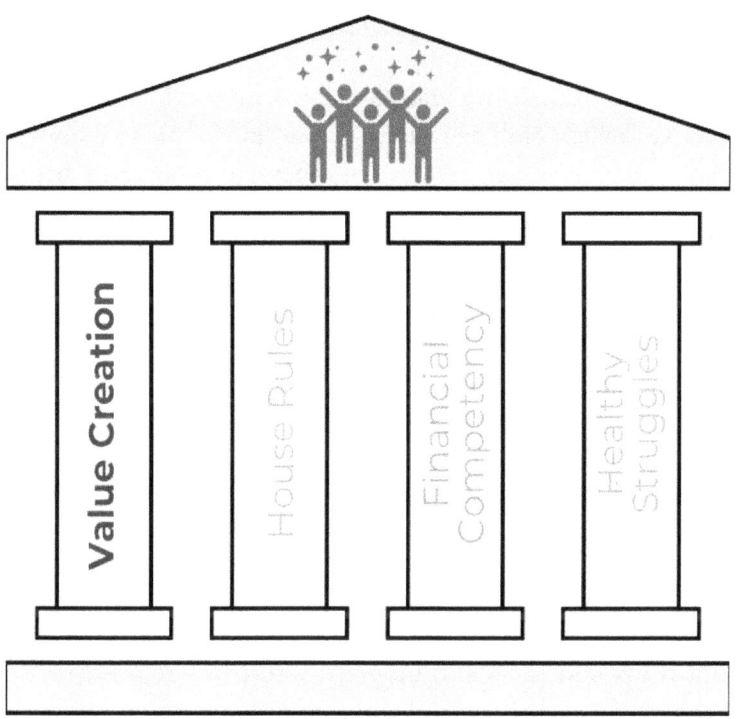

MATERIAL VALUE CREATION

In many families, money seems to be the biggest focus when it comes to value creation. It can also be a source of much anxiety and stress. Even those who say money isn't that important frequently act in ways that say the opposite.

Growing up in my family, I observed that money dominated decisions, actions, and behaviors. Probably because we didn't have much of it. My parents focused more on gaming government programs to generate income over earning income by creating value in the world. As a result, they placed little focus and value on creating positive emotional energy or spiritual value within the family.

If unaddressed, we will pass down unhealthy and unproductive beliefs and behaviors to our kids. I have observed these unproductive beliefs and behaviors passed to my siblings, along with the challenges they have endured in life as a result. It is never too late to work on addressing these things.

> IN MANY FAMILIES, MONEY SEEMS TO BE THE BIGGEST FOCUS WHEN IT COMES TO VALUE CREATION. IT CAN ALSO BE A SOURCE OF MUCH ANXIETY AND STRESS. EVEN THOSE WHO SAY MONEY ISN'T THAT IMPORTANT FREQUENTLY ACT IN WAYS THAT SAY THE OPPOSITE.

I have a close relationship with my sister, who is a year and a half older than I. She has two kids and four grandkids. A couple of years ago, I started working closely with my sister to change the way she, her daughter, and her grandkids think and feel about money. I wanted to help even more because of the challenging living conditions for her grandkids.

For my sister, her grandkids are her world. These four kids have three different fathers and a mother experiencing many personal struggles. One of the fathers has been out of the picture for years and still is. My niece often would work all day and late into the night, come home to sleep a couple of hours, then leave again, but my sister was and is always there for the children. They were living in tight living quarters where the power was regularly turned off from not paying the bill. I made a deal with my sister that I would help by renting a house where all of the kids and grandma would have their own rooms, but I had conditions. She had to implement the Dinner Table Method[IP] in the family. This was difficult for her because she is very proud and does not like to accept help.

Per these conditions, I agreed to cover the cost of the home and certain bills, and my sister would own building emotional energy and spiritual (connectedness) value for the family. It has been interesting and wonderful to watch the transition. At first, my sister actually said she felt like a loser because she was accepting money from me when she should be able to provide on her own.

As we talked more about the three categories of value creation and how they apply to the family, it started to sink in. I made the case that what I was contributing on the material value side (money) wasn't nearly as valuable as what she was contributing by creating emotional (energy) and spiritual value (connectedness) for the family. In this scenario, my sister is creating more value for the family than I am. Now she is owning her job for the family with a strong sense of pride. And importantly, she no longer feels like a loser when it comes to money.

We continue to make significant progress with her grandkids regarding their relationship with money as well. The kids are six, ten, thirteen, and sixteen. We have lots of conversations around money. The ability to create material value (earn money) is an important ability for all kids and adults to develop throughout their lives. Money is nothing more than a tool to sustain a lifestyle and make a difference in the world. It is not good or bad. How we earn it and deploy it is up to each individual, family, and organization.

How we talk about material value creation within the family is so important.

- How do you earn it?
- What does it take to earn more of it?
- How do you deploy it?
- How do you feel about it?
- How do you feel about those who have it and those who do not?

These conversations can form our kids' emotional and practical application relationship with money for the rest of their lives.

The best long-term strategy for earning more and more money, if that is important to you, is to make every transaction a win-win. This has been my strategy for decades, and it has really paid off. If earning money is an exchange of value, then it is important for both sides of that transaction to win. If one side loses, they will likely not return, shutting that door to future earning opportunities.

Having a win-win approach has worked well for me. Doing my best to ensure that all stakeholders win in every transaction has exposed me to many more opportunities than those with a win-lose approach will ever have. Even as a kid, it was important to me that I delivered more value than I was paid. It meant they would ask me back, it gave better job security, and it always exposed me to the next opportunity.

> DOING MY BEST TO ENSURE THAT ALL STAKEHOLDERS WIN IN EVERY TRANSACTION HAS EXPOSED ME TO MANY MORE OPPORTUNITIES THAN THOSE WITH A WIN-LOSE APPROACH WILL EVER HAVE.

Those with more of a win-lose approach to earning money, or not delivering the value they agreed to for what they were paid, will usually stay stuck when it comes to earning more money. Over the years, I occasionally had employees who wanted more money and, at the same time, asked to do less to earn it. In those cases, I would usually help them get a job at one of my competitors. Employees who got the most raises and advancement opportunities were those who regularly asked, "What else can I do?"

Making money is just one of three categories of creating value, but it is an important one. Sustaining our lifestyle and having the resources to make a difference in the world matters. I think of my money in savings and other assets as my accumulated best efforts. When I work for someone, I am exchanging my best efforts for some of their accumulated best efforts.

There is no end to our ability to increase the value we create and earn more. Increasing the amount of money earned takes effort and can be hard work. It can also be fun and rewarding with the right mindset. How you talk about money with your kids now will really matter when they become adults.

Material value creation (making money) may be a budding superpower for one or more of your kids. Expose them to opportunities to earn money, including what it looks like to start and run a business. If they seem to "get it" and talk about where it could go, they may have a superpower waiting to be developed.

When I was thirteen, my stepfather had started a sign-painting business. He was a very talented artist. One day, he showed me where he was set up in a warehouse doing his painting. He explained that he got paid for each sign he painted, and he had quite a few Union 76 gas station signs waiting to be delivered. Then he showed me an area where he was setting up silk-screening that would allow him to paint ten of the same signs in the time it took him to paint one by hand. And he would be paid the same for each sign! I instantly understood, and my brain started obsessing about how to get more customers, create more signs, and experience exponential growth.

The business never took off for my stepfather, but ever since then, I've had the bug to start a business. This led to starting many businesses; I'm sure I'll create many more in the future too. This is just one small example to help you look for material value-creation superpowers in your own kids.

EMOTIONAL VALUE CREATION

When I reflect on what made me successful as a kid and young adult, emotional energy was the key. So much so that when people ask me what the scarcest commodity on the planet is, I always say *positive emotional energy*. I would rather live half as long with my emotional energy at 9 or 10 on a scale from 1–10, than twice as long at 1 or 2. Positive emotional energy supercharges everything we do, and it significantly enriches our experiences.

It has been fun to watch the fast transformation in kids when the concept of emotional energy value is introduced within a family. It's more than just asking, "How do you think that made your sister or brother feel?" That is important, for sure. Bigger picture, it is now seen as a way to create value for the family and help each kid create more value for themselves.

A mother in our Dinner Table Family community shared a story after only a few months of implementing the Dinner Table Method within their home. She walked in on one of her kids folding the laundry. When she asked why she was doing the laundry when it was Mom's job, her daughter said, "I am doing the laundry so you can spend time with my younger sister to create emotional and spiritual value." Wow!

Emotional energy is the mood, attitude, and feelings we bring to our interactions. It is shaped by how we think and feel about ourselves and others. For example, when some people walk into a room, they "light it up." People want to be around that person and interact with them. The opposite is also true. If someone enters a room filled with negative emotional energy, the whole "vibe" of the room can change for the worse.

When positive emotional energy is high, family members feel more connected, motivated, and supported. On the other hand, negative emotional energy can lead to tension, misunderstandings, and disconnection. Understanding the significance of emotional energy is the first step to fostering a value-creation-focused home environment.

Although our emotional energy affects others, understanding it begins within ourselves. A good question is: How does it make me feel to elevate others or bring them down? Once family members become aware of their emotional impact on others, they can more intentionally elevate positive emotional energy.

Some kids have a superpower when it comes to emotional energy. You can see it in how they light up a room with their energy and personality. Usually, when this is the case, they can also take a room down just as fast. Once kids are aware of this superpower, they can be much more intentional about how they use it to create value.

If emotional energy is a superpower for certain kids, it can help guide what they want to do for a living when they become adults. Positive emotional energy is the X-factor for leaders within organizations. Going down the leadership path is one way to leverage this superpower when your kids start their careers. There are many other ways, including writing, performing, speaking, acting, and more.

Of the three categories of value creation, I believe emotional energy is my strongest. I was well into adulthood before I realized the effect my energy had on individuals and groups of people. From that point on, I became very intentional about not letting a low emotional energy day affect the people I interacted with. I even developed an internal mantra for my low emotional energy days: Be *your best when you are at your worst.*

As a kid, I loved playing guitar. I started playing so young, I don't remember *not* knowing how to play guitar. Music is a wonderful way to express positive emotional energy. It always uplifted me personally and those I performed for. Imagine if one of your kids performs or writes a song that uplifts a crowd. This is creating positive emotional energy value in the world. Imagine if this song becomes popular and millions or more listen to it and are uplifted emotionally as a result.

Music is a personal favorite of mine when it comes to conveying positive emotional energy in the world. I graduated from high school in 1980. In the first half of that decade, my band performed over one thousand nights. This was how I earned most of my money back then. Playing guitar for me was about expressing emotion through every note I played.

It still is.

In my opinion, there is no end to how well this can be done. There is literally an infinite number of ways to play a single note on the guitar. The same applies to singing a note. You can listen to one hundred accomplished singers sing the same song, and sometimes only one of them will move you deeply. They all sing the same notes and on pitch, but one more effectively connected their emotions to the notes.

Once I realized positive emotional energy was such an advantage in leadership, I leaned in to leverage it in a win-win way there too. Leadership is creating value with and through others. Through that lens, we are all leaders, and we can choose to develop it at the pace we are comfortable with. For example, when kids get their first job, they are creating value with others. If they choose, they can become a supervisor or manager, creating even more value through others.

> ONCE I REALIZED POSITIVE EMOTIONAL ENERGY WAS SUCH AN ADVANTAGE IN LEADERSHIP, I LEANED IN TO LEVERAGE IT IN A WIN-WIN WAY THERE TOO. LEADERSHIP IS CREATING VALUE WITH AND THROUGH OTHERS.

Emotional energy doesn't have to be a superpower for your kids to leverage it to create more value for themselves or the family. Being aware of it and its value is a powerful first step. It can be cultivated into a superpower for any kid (or adult) who puts in the effort.

One thing worth mentioning is the impact health and fitness have on your emotional energy. For me, this is a powerful hack to maintain emotional energy higher than it would be otherwise, given life's changing conditions. Simplifying my approach to health and fitness boils down to *nourish-right*, *move-right*, and *recover-right*[TP]. At least, that is how I think about it. When I don't do these three things consistently well, it can lower my emotional energy two to three points on a scale from 1 to 10.

I believe the brain is the most important organ in our body. In Daniel G. Amen's books, *Change Your Brain Every Day* and *Change Your Brain, Change Your Life*, he lays out solid strategies for taking care of and optimizing your brain's function. Following these strategies will make it much easier to sustain a high level of positive emotional energy.

SPIRITUAL VALUE CREATION

Spiritual value creation, at its core, is about connectedness. It is not the same as spirituality or religion, but these can be an important part of spiritual value creation if a family or individual chooses them to be. Within the family, it starts with your kids being connected with themselves, understanding how they think and feel. From there, it goes to how connected your family members are with each other. This can expand to communities, work, school, church, a higher power, or whatever is important to your family. Strong connections are essential for personal fulfillment and societal and family well-being.

Like most things, it is important to be intentional in your conversations about spiritual value creation. I like starting with what it means to be part of the family. What is your family history? Include the good along with the challenges that form the emotional connection with where your family is today. How are you talking about this as a family?

Some families have amazing histories that keep building on what it means to be in the family generationally. Others can be hot messes. It really doesn't matter because you can build something amazing starting from where you are if you choose to do so. And there is no end to how you can strengthen family connections and a sense of family pride. (Think back to chapter 1, "The Best Time to Begin is Now.")

As I mentioned earlier, the family environment in which I grew up fell into the hot mess category. As a result, I have chosen a new family over the years from people I met along the way. I have a few sets of informally adopted parents and kids that I love very much. And there are many I consider brothers and sisters. We would all run through walls for each other. These relationships span as far back as fifty years for me.

I haven't given up on my biological family, and it has been fulfilling to rebuild with my sister, her kids, and grandkids. To develop deeper connections, we gather once a month for conversations about everyone's job for the family, progress toward family goals, the kids' interests, and more. This reinforces keeping up the Dinner Table Method when we are not all together. And of course, several calls each week to check in.

We have established a ritual of going on a family vacation at the start of each summer. Our most recent trip was to Yellowstone National Park. But let me backtrack a bit before continuing.

VALUE CREATION FAMILY

One of the things we do as a team sport and to strengthen family connections is to get all the kids involved in the household budget. Each of the kids, even the six-year-old, has a line item on the budget. Hers is the Dutch Brothers budget. She and her two sisters love getting hot drinks from there.

Once they saw how much they were spending, they chose to buy the ingredients and make the tea and coffee drinks at home, saving over 50 percent! They got so good at finding savings just about everywhere on the family budget that they beat the budget five months in a row. The kids asked if they could use the money they saved for the family vacation, and they picked Yellowstone National Park. They love the outdoors and are leaning toward Yosemite National Park for our next trip.

How sneaky of me to make household budgeting a team family sport! I let the kids and my sister, who has never been good with money, struggle through developing this skill, and they all have gotten good at it. And now, they are allocating surplus to vacations. These days, when I ask my sister if she is good when it comes to money, she just smiles and says yes. It was never like this before. She even takes five percent of the total household income and puts it in savings—the first line item on the family budget.

Doing this together really helped strengthen our family relationships, and financial skills were developed that weren't there before. This has been a big step in starting to remove the unhealthy relationship my family has historically had with money. And the kids can't stop talking about our time in Yellowstone and planning for our next trip. I can't wait for the next trip either. We had so much fun!

Working on this as a family, along with many other things, is building on what it means to be part of our family. Now, when we talk about the challenging stories from our past, we reflect on what we learned that can help us today and in the future. I see an amazing future for my family starting from where we are today. Even in an unhealthy struggle, there is value to be created.

Building connectedness through community can be powerful and life-changing. There are so many opportunities to do this. One community I have been a part of for many years is the ITF Taekwon-Do community. In my late twenties, I started studying under Grandmaster Sun Duk Choi, who was a student of General Choi Hung Hi, the founder of the ITF (International Taekwon-Do Federation).

After reaching the rank of Fourth Degree black belt, I opened my own full-time Taekwon-Do school in Scottsdale, Arizona. I taught for about twenty-three years before I stopped in 2016 as a Sixth Degree. I poured a lot into this community over the years, and to this day, I have not lost my connection. I am sponsoring seven students to compete in the 2025 World competition in Croatia. I have made many life-long Taekwon-Do friends and can go just about anywhere in the world and stay with one of my Taekwon-Do brothers and sisters.

I can't overstate the power of leaning in to help communities that are important to you create value. Every time I do it, and there have been many, I am exposed to opportunities I couldn't see before. These include job opportunities, investments, friendships, and much more. For this to work, you have to show up to make a difference. It won't work if you show up only to get something without giving.

Strengthening connectedness with our family, individuals, and communities requires leaning in to being there for each other on this amazing journey. Healthy connections and relationships are earned. Like the old saying goes, "You get out of it what you put into it." For me, the rewards have been incredibly fulfilling.

BIGGEST TAKEAWAYS FROM CHAPTER 2:

- Unhealthy emotions surrounding money can be passed to future generations.
- Look for signs of hidden value-creation superpowers within your kids.
- Money is nothing more than accumulated best efforts that can be used to exchange value.
- Being aware of the impact of positive and negative emotional energy is a powerful tool for your kids to create value for themselves and the family.
- Consider positive emotional energy as one of the world's scarcest commodities.
- Nourish-right, move-right, recover-right.
- Spiritual value creation, at its core, is about connectedness.
- Connectedness starts with your kids exploring and understanding why they think and feel the way they do.
- Being part of a community will pay significant spiritual value-creation returns if you put in the work.

Chapter 3

CREATING HOUSE RULES LEADS TO BETTER RELATIONSHIPS

Households Run Better When Everyone Is Doing What Is Expected of Them

The second pillar of the Dinner Table Method is House Rules. Households run better when everyone is doing what is expected of them. Another way to frame this is that everybody has a job for the family. In the beginning, these jobs are often not clearly defined or implemented. But when done right, it can free up a lot of time for parents to create even more value for the family.

I have the pleasure and honor of leading several Dinner Table Family communities. We've seen a powerful pattern. When kids are given a clear job for the family, they own it quickly and with a sense of pride. This is especially true when they can see that the rest of the family members also have a clearly-defined job for the family, and they are doing their part.

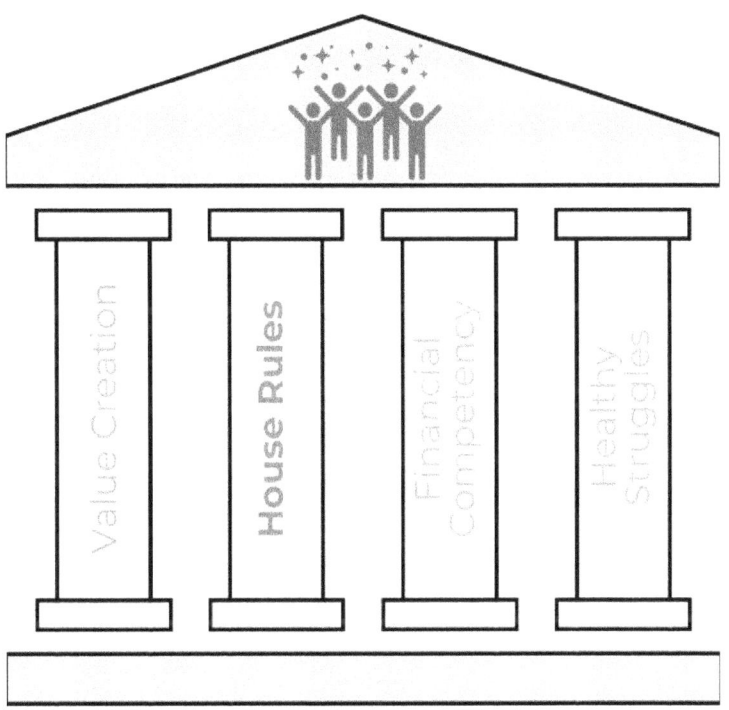

How you set up the conversation to create jobs for the family is important. This helps them understand why they should do it. Start by setting goals for the family. Begin slowly and give family members time to get in the groove. Once you have established family goals, creating everyone's job for the family as a way of helping achieve your family goals makes more sense.

Do you set goals as a family? If so, do you regularly follow up? Setting goals usually isn't the hard part. Following up and accomplishing them is.

Following up can be as simple as talking about the family goals and their progress once a month at the dinner table.

- Are we on track?
- Are we stuck anywhere?
- How can we work better together to achieve these goals?

A few of the common short- and long-term family goals we hear from our Dinner Table community families include:

- **Short term:**
    - Finding steady, reliable employment
    - Getting children to take ownership of household chores
    - For our kids to be confident and capable
    - 10 percent or more additional family income
    - Set and stick to a family budget
    - Find ways to save on household expenses
    - Having enough money in savings to cover all the bills for at least six months
    - Move into a new house
    - Additional car

- **Long term:**
    - To be healthy, happy, and fulfilled
    - To ensure our kids have the character and capabilities to be successful adults
    - To be able to afford the right education for our kids that will allow them to create value in the world, the way they want to
    - Kids are ready to take on responsibility for the family in the event that something happens to one or both parents
    - To pass our family legacy to our kids and equip them to build on it generationally

Take some time to write down a few short- and long-term goals for the family. There should be goals on the list that benefit every family member. Then set time aside to discuss and refine the goals with the entire family. Set expectations so that everyone understands that, as the family evolves, the goals may change as well. I recommend at least a monthly check-in on the list with the entire family. Schedule it so it happens. For example, make the first Sunday dinner of each month a family goals discussion around the dinner table.

You will have a much higher chance of achieving your family goals if everyone is doing their job for the family, including your kids. Kids doing their job for the family does not mean they get paid for it. These expectations are their contribution to the family. This can start as early as age three and include putting away their toys, brushing their teeth, being kind to their siblings, and so on. These jobs for the family will change as they get older.

It is also helpful for you, as a parent or guardian, to list your job for the family, with a high-level description for each expectation. They can include:

- Provide income to support the family lifestyle
- Create and maintain the family budget
- Model a healthy relationship
- Maintain open communication and be a safe space
- Establish routines and provide structure
- Actively participate in your kids' lives
- Model character traits and beliefs that are beneficial to pass to your kids

Once you have created your initial set of family value-creation goals and each family member's job for the family, it is helpful to find a place in the house to display them.

The following graphic (Figure 2) shows an example of family value-creation goals in the center, and each family member's job for the family, with expectations listed around the goals.

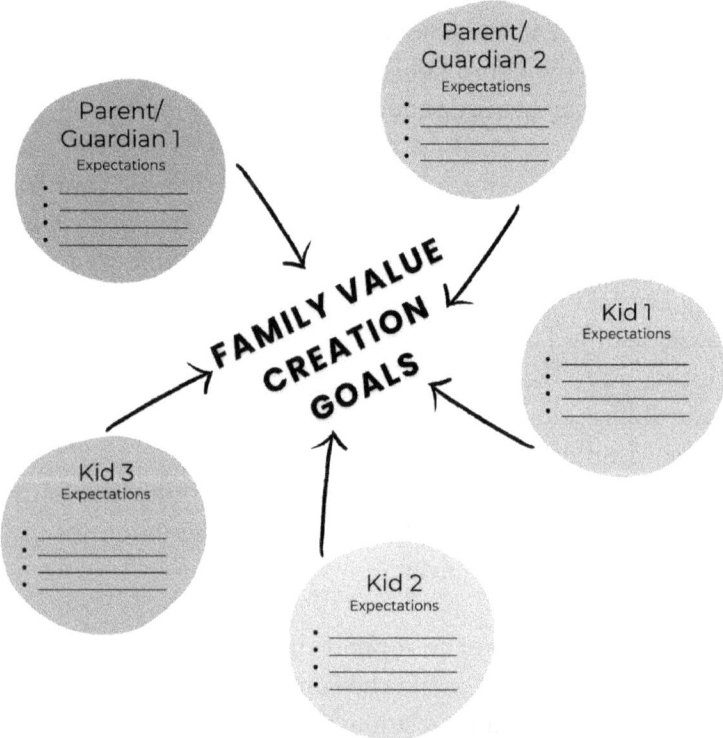

Figure 2. Creating family goals.

With the family goals and each family member's expectations listed around them for all to see, it is a great way to visualize how your family creates value as a unit. You can hold each other accountable in a respectful way and help each other out when picking up the slack as needed due to unforeseen circumstances.

A next step is listing each of your kids' short- and long-term goals and displaying those as well. Effective goal setting can take some time to get good at it. The important part is to start. Even if it takes a year for your kids to get good at setting goals, it will be a valuable life skill to have when they become adults. This is true especially since many adults today are not very good at setting goals.

Short-term and long-term goals will change significantly for your kids as they get older. For your kids under ten years old, ask what they would like to accomplish in the next couple of months for their short-term goals. For their long-term goals, ask what they would like to accomplish in the next year or two. Always do this through the lens of, "How do you want to create value in the world now and as you get older?" Be patient as they develop their ability to think through and build this capability.

For your kids ten years old or older, ask what they would like to accomplish in the next twelve months for their short-term goals. For their long-term goals, ask them what they would like to accomplish by the time they become an adult at eighteen. Encourage them to incorporate strengthening character, capabilities, and beliefs into their goals.

Starting the Dinner Table Method with your kids early is ideal, but you can begin at any age. My experience has shown that the earlier you start, the faster the adoption will occur. Starting later, at the age of fifteen, for example, can often initially appear as if they want nothing to do with any of this. Fast forward a year, and more often than not, they are owning most, if not all, of it. Patience and monitoring for progress are required.

A key to making this work is to be consistent as parents. Have set times to discuss family and individual goals. Don't do too much of the work for your kids. Let them struggle some in order to develop character traits and capabilities. Allowing for this healthy struggle will shape their beliefs around what is possible. (More on the value of struggle in chapter 5.)

A foundational job for all kids' journey in the family is to earn, manage, and appreciate the value of money. If not, they will be missing a crucial component required to be a successful adult. In the Dinner Table Method, we break it down into what we call the three Es:

1. Expectations
2. Earning money
3. Expenses

Let's unpack these one at a time.

1. EXPECTATIONS

Expectations outline each of your kids' jobs for the family. They do not get paid an allowance for this; rather, it's their contribution to the family.

If you had to hire out what your kids do for the family, it would cost something. This is real value they are contributing to the family. Adding this perspective when discussing everyone's job for the family adds to understanding and appreciating the value of money.

2. EARNING MONEY

For your kids to learn how to manage and understand the value of money more fully, they will need to earn money. Earning money will have to be based on doing things on top of their job for the family. Your kids' options for earning money will change as they get older. Early on, they can earn money doing gigs at home. As the kids get older, they can do community gigs outside the home and eventually get a job to earn money. *Gigs* sound better than *chores* to me. There are two categories of gigs. Action gigs and brain gigs.

Action gigs can include washing the car, organizing the garage, deep-cleaning a room, and more.

Brain gigs include learning anything that can be applied to create value.

Action Gig examples:

- Mow the lawn
- Power-wash the outside of the house
- Maintain a preventative maintenance schedule for the home and ensure all maintenance is done on time
- Organize and clean tools in the garage
- Help your siblings with their homework

Brain Gig examples:

- Read a book and report on or demonstrate how what you learned can be applied to create value
- Research a subject and report on or demonstrate how what you learned can be applied to create value
- Interview someone you admire and report on or demonstrate how what you learned can be applied to create value

There are hundreds of ways kids can earn money in a safe and effective way. When you are paying your kids to do home gigs, make sure to never pay them more than you would pay someone else to do a particular gig. You are teaching your kids the value of money. Overpaying will give them a distorted view of what they should earn for the value they are providing. For example, if you could get your car washed at the local carwash for eight dollars, don't pay your kid twenty-five dollars to wash it. I suggest that if you can get your car washed at the carwash for eight dollars, then offer it to your kids for six dollars, since there are the added water and soap costs when doing it at home.

Here is a funny story from a recent Dinner Table community session I was facilitating on this topic. One of the mothers brought up that her husband had dishwashing duty certain nights of the week. To get out of it, he would pay one of their kids twenty dollars to do the dishes. It only takes twenty minutes at the most. She then said she would do the dishes and that he should pay her twenty dollars. The room burst out laughing! The point? Dad was way overpaying for what, at most, should have been a five-dollar job.

One of the families in our community living in the Boston area came up with a creative way to give action gigs to their two girls, eight and eleven years old. Mom and Dad would make a list of several small gigs that needed to be done around the house. They would write the gig on a sticky note, attach it to a one- or two-dollar bill, and clip all the gigs to a string hanging from a window. The girls simply unclip a note, do the gig, and pocket the money. They sent me a picture of three gigs hanging in this fashion. They were:

1. Empty the dishwasher and reload with dirty dishes for two dollars.
2. Dust the floor heaters and baseboards for one dollar, with the added note, I will show you how.
3. Fold the laundry and put it in the rooms for one dollar.

This is so creative and fun!

3. EXPENSES

Once your kids start picking up some of their own expenses, they really start to learn the value of money. This can start as early as eight to ten years old by having your kids pay for birthday gifts for friends and siblings. As they get older, they can pick up the cost of movies and activities with their friends. From there, they can use their earnings for car expenses (if they have one), such as gas and insurance. Some parents have even had their older kids pay for filling cavities, so they learn how important it is to take care of their teeth by flossing and brushing daily.

Everything in this chapter helps your kids create value for the family and prepare them for adulthood. I always make a point when working with my sister and her grandkids to thank them for doing their job for the family. And I will also ask, from time to time, how doing their job for the family will help them be successful when they become an adult.

Creating value for the family and readiness for adulthood are two foundational touchstones. Keeping these things front of mind helps me be keenly intentional in preparing kids for a successful launch into adulthood.

BIGGEST TAKEAWAYS FROM CHAPTER 3:

- Set goals as a family and follow up consistently
- Set individual goals for family members and follow up consistently
- Create each family member's job for the family, with a list of expectations for each job
- Create an environment where kids can earn money in a fair exchange of value way

- Have kids pick up some of their expenses early and increase them as they get older
- Creating value for the family and readiness for adulthood are two foundational touchstones

Chapter 4

BUILD YOUR KIDS' FINANCIAL COMPETENCY

Create an Environment Where Your Kids Understand Money

The third pillar of the Dinner Table Method is Financial Competency. Being financially competent when you become an adult is one of the most important foundational capabilities to have. There is a lot of talk about financial literacy, but financial literacy doesn't matter if you don't know how to apply these concepts to sustain your lifestyle in a responsible way.

I graduated from high school in 1980. Even then, we were not taught financial literacy or money skills in K-12 public education. I was really good at earning money by the time I was kicked out of the house. However, I was not good at managing it to ensure I could sustain my lifestyle and plan for the unexpected. This was an authentic trial by fire for me.

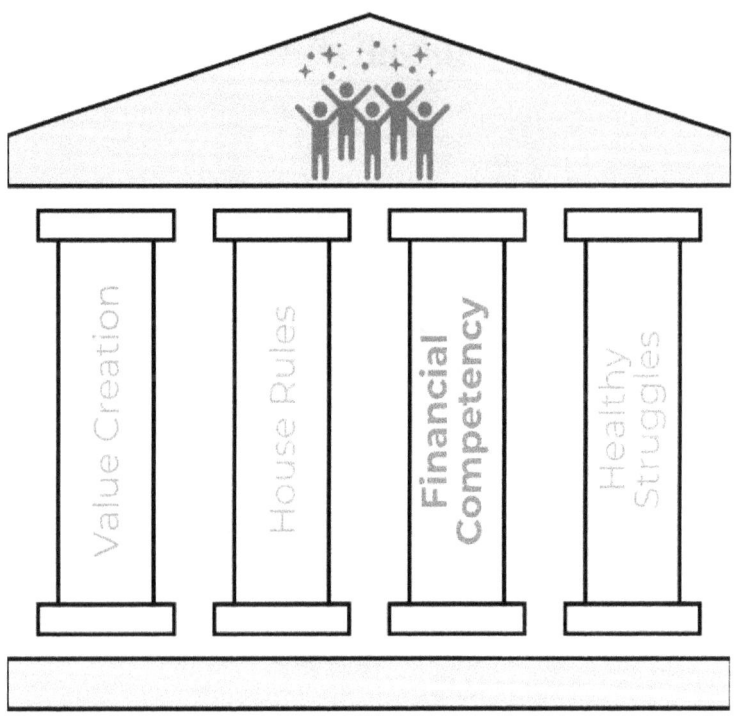

Until that point, my thoughts were around earning more money to buy guitars, pay for my truck expenses, and engage in my other hobbies, including racing motorcycles. Once I was on my own, other thoughts immediately flooded in: *I can't lose my job, what if I have an unexpected medical expense, I now have to buy all of my own food, I can't spend all of my paycheck every time I get it,* and more. The weight of having to be fully responsible for myself financially hit me instantly. I had no choice. It was quite the emotional struggle as I was settling into my new life condition. And, it was one of the best things that ever happened to me.

I remember taking earning money for granted because I seemed to find work as a teenager easily. Once I was kicked out of the house, I developed some insecurities around this because I couldn't afford to lose my income stream. I think this made me more valuable to the places I worked because I tried even harder to demonstrate the value I was contributing in exchange for my paycheck. It was surprising at the time, but about a week after being on my own, my manager at the Coco's Restaurant where I worked said there was something different about me in a really positive way. Even though I didn't think anyone else would notice, he did. I had a stronger sense of responsibility, accountability, and appreciation for my employment opportunity.

Today, I have enough money to cover my living expenses and lifestyle for as long as I live, even if I never earn another dollar. This includes giving a significant amount of money each year to causes that are important to me. I have fully earned all of this over decades of hard and smart work, and it is a rewarding and fulfilling accomplishment for me. It is much easier to fully focus on making a positive difference in the world when you don't have financial worries.

Even with where I am today financially, I have no trouble remembering what it was like to live on the edge financially in the first few years on my own. I fought to hold on to every dollar I earned because I had to. To save money, there were weeks during my senior year in high school when all I had to eat was a jar of peanut butter and a loaf of white bread. Sometimes I would splurge and add honey to the peanut butter sandwich. I remember it tasting really good! Even though things were tight, after a few months, I got into the groove and knew I would be able to survive this experience. What a sense of accomplishment I felt as the only kid in my high school living on my own!

Which money skills and in what order of importance do you want your kids to develop before becoming adults? What do you think they are capable of when it comes to financial competency and independence? How long will the bank of Mom and Dad be open for non-emergency needs for your kids? I know many young adults still being supported by their parents in their late twenties, and some well into their thirties. Okay, and a few in their forties and fifties!

Every year, I hear more adults saying kids can't be expected to do this or that. And the list keeps growing. Why would we tell kids they can do anything they set their mind and efforts to and at the same time tell them what they can't be expected to do at their age? An example of this is the lack of belief in today's culture that kids can be financially competent and independent when they turn eighteen years old. I was fully financially independent at seventeen. One of my business partners also fully supported himself financially at seventeen. I knew lots of kids back in the late seventies and early eighties who accomplished this. It was more the norm back then.

What changed in a generation or two?

I don't believe anyone fully knows what is possible in terms of the value they can create. And for sure, I believe kids can do so much more than most adults believe they can. We can make lots of excuses and point to reasons as to why we, with the best of intentions, infuse these limiting beliefs in our kids.

MONEY SKILLS

There are eight money skills. I believe you need to put them in the order of importance for you and your family. This is the order of my list:

1. Earn
2. Protect

3. Save
4. Budget
5. Spend
6. Share
7. Invest
8. Borrow

Proficiency at each of these money skills leads to financial competence. And all of these skills should be applied with a value-creation mindset. It would be easy to write an entire book on each of these skills (and many have). My intent here is to primarily capture why each is important and lead you to think about desired outcomes. You don't have to be an expert on each of these skills; just make them work for you.

EARNING MONEY

Earning money is getting paid for the value you create. This could be within an organization or directly for a customer. It can be from an organization you work for or own. If one of your kids sets up a lemonade stand selling directly to customers, this is a mini business, and such a great learning opportunity. The reason I put earning at the top of the list of money skills is that you must have money to apply all of the other money skills. And in the material-value creation category, it has been helpful in teaching me how to grow the value I create in exchange for money.

When I was ten, I wandered the neighborhood knocking on doors, asking if I could mow their lawns in the summer and shovel their driveways and walkways in the winter. This was my little one-kid business. I also had a number of paper routes where I would get up super early to deliver the *Spokane*

Review newspaper to over one hundred homes before going to school. In this case, I was paid by an organization for the value I created for them. Over time, I got really good tips for placing the newspapers exactly where the homeowners wanted and by the time they expected it to be there. I collected the money door-to-door for their subscriptions on a monthly basis. This was a great way for me to learn customer service and general people skills.

My attitude was that I would do just about anything to earn money as a kid, as long as it was moral and legal. I would do any odd job, no matter how hot or dirty the conditions were. As I mentioned previously, I got my start pulling weeds for twenty-five cents an hour at the age of six. I encourage this willingness to start earning money with all of the kids I work with. You can start anywhere and go everywhere with the right mindset, work ethic, and discipline.

I was having a conversation with a sixteen-year-old girl in our Dinner Table community about options to earn money. She was setting goals that would set her up to live on her own when she turned eighteen. She was stuck on where to start, thinking her only option was to work at a fast-food restaurant. I told her I thought this was a great option for a first job. She will learn many valuable skills, as I did, working in a restaurant at her age. Then I suggested we make a broader list of potential options.

She was an artist and loved painting. I suggested charging money for a fun group-painting class, and she lit up. We also discussed working in retail, hospitality, personal shopping, driving the elderly to appointments, organizing closets, tutoring younger kids, and many other options. There are hundreds of options for kids to earn money at various ages. They often just need a little brainstorming help from friends and adults to open up the possibilities. Then, sit back and enjoy watching them apply their youthful energy to creating value in exchange for money. As a parent, you serve as a sounding board on their journey, letting them know that struggle is good and expected as they learn to create more value.

In a company I sold in 2016, we had a sizable engineering department. This company was called Able Aerospace, and we repaired, overhauled, and manufactured aircraft components for around two thousand customers who supported or operated aircraft in sixty countries. Out of five hundred employees, about 10 percent were in engineering positions.

I remember interviewing a recent college grad student for an engineering position. He wanted $111,000 as a starting salary. When I asked where he came up with that number, he said this is what his college said he should expect going into his first engineering job. I then asked how much value he would create to justify this salary, explaining that he needs to create more than he is being paid for it to make sense. When you include benefits and matching taxes, the total cost to the company would be around $140,000, so he would need to create in the neighborhood of $200,000 in value each year. He actually said he didn't care, and if we wanted to hire him, we had to pay what he was asking. He expected us to pay for his degree, not the value he could create. I handed him a list of our competitors and wished him luck.

Understanding how you create value for the organization you work for and always ensuring you are creating more than you are being paid will put you in the upper 5 percent of team members. Infusing a value-creation mindset in your kids will give them a big advantage in any organization when they start their careers.

PROTECTING YOUR MONEY

I put protecting money as the second money skill because as soon as you earn some money, there are so many ways people will try to take it from you. It doesn't matter how little or how much you have. Possessing this money skill is about being aware and smart when it comes to reading others' intentions and keeping your money safe.

Access to your money was an early lesson I learned the hard way as a kid. I would have my paychecks deposited into my checking account and use my bank debit card to purchase things. I liked it because it made it easy to track and organize expenses each month. The problem was that wherever I used it, the merchant would have access to my debit card number, and in the first year of doing this, my bank account was drained twice by someone nefariously using my account number. I quickly switched to a credit card after the second time, and if there was ever a charge I didn't approve, I could dispute it. I never again had my bank account drained this way.

My parents having access to my social security number and other personal information made it easy for them to rack up credit card debt in my name. This taught me the importance of protecting my personal information by the time I was eighteen. Today, I recommend that everyone lock their credit reports so that creditors can access to see your credit history. In the United States, they are Equifax, Experian, and TransUnion.

When it comes time to apply for a loan or credit facility like a credit card or home equity line of credit (HELOC), simply unlock the creditor's desired credit reporting agency for that transaction. No legitimate lender will grant credit without access to your credit history through one of these agencies. I had a credit union contact me recently requesting that I unlock my credit report so they could approve my loan, and I had never applied for that loan!

From the day I started making money, my friends would ask to borrow it. To this day, I only have one instance where the money I lent to a friend was paid back. Decades ago, I developed a policy whereby I would never loan money to friends. If I had it and thought it would truly help, I would give it to them in cases of real emergencies. A friend needing money to make a rent payment while at the same time living way outside their means is not an emergency. They need to change their spending habits. Loaning or giving money in these situations enables a person's poor financial decision-making to continue. Not to mention that loaning money to friends is a proven way to mess up a friendship.

Giving to nonprofits is another trap to watch out for. All nonprofits have what appears to be a noble mission, like saving animals, feeding people, fighting human trafficking, environmental causes, and more. I have learned the hard way to not take their word on the impact they say they are having.

When you really dig in, most of the time, they do not have anywhere near the impact they claim. You may feel good giving to a cause that is important to you, but I recommend making sure your money is being used the way you want. It's important to protect yourself from disingenuous messaging from nonprofits not delivering on the impact that snagged your attention. Unfortunately, my experience has shown me that many nonprofits do not deliver on their stated impact. Regarding these, most have good intentions, but they are not capable. And of course, there are some that are flat-out unethical and deceptive.

My desired outcome from protecting my money is to keep it safe from hackers and fraudsters. And to have the emotional toughness to say no to friends, family, and causes where giving money won't really help. Sometimes giving money can make things worse for the receiver over time.

SAVING MONEY

Saving money is a mindset that most kids and adults don't have. Too many families live on the edge with little to no savings. As of this writing, 29 percent of Americans have less than three months of expenses in savings. And 27 percent of Americans have no emergency savings. To be financially responsible, I believe we should all have at least six months of our total expenses in savings. Here is a breakdown of Americans with six months or more of their approximate monthly expenses in savings:

- Gen X   (age 45–60)   **20%**
- Millennials   (age 29–44)   **25%**
- Gen Z   (age 18–28)   **10%**

For sure, there are hardship cases where having significant savings is difficult to achieve. However, I think the primary reason for such a low savings rate in the United States is two-fold. One, not thinking through and understanding the long-term value of saving money. And two, poor decision-making when it comes to living within a person's means.

I loved the feeling I had the first time I had saved more than six months of expenses in my savings account. Recently, I had coffee with a long-time friend in her forties who reached having a year's worth of expenses in savings this past year. She went on about how good it made her feel. She talked about spending money to remodel her home, and it didn't stress her out like spending money on these things would have in the past. And all while still growing her savings.

It's helpful to talk about savings goals as a family. This is great training for kids to develop a savings mindset. Understanding this value will go with them into adulthood.

Savings goals vary greatly from family to family. Here are a few categories for family savings goals that I think about. Savings can:

- cover unexpected expenses and emergencies
- cover living expenses in case of income disruption
- pay for kids' college expenses
- pay for home preventative maintenance, taxes, and other expenses
- pay for family vacations
- pay for hobbies
- support causes important to you and your family
- cover my lifestyle when I can't or choose to no longer work
- leave something to your family when you are gone, and distribute it responsibly

There is significant value in growing a family's savings, including reduced stress, preparing for the future, and the ability to take advantage of smart investment opportunities, among other benefits. Growing savings is a long-term play. If we don't do it right, we will be in for quite the financial shock when retirement comes around!

Living within a family's means seems to be a real challenge. Why do so many suffer from what I call "I have it, therefore I must spend it." The expression "money burning a hole in your pocket" is metaphorically true for most people. Saving a percentage of your income should be the first line item on your budget. And for additional savings, we should always look for ways to enjoy our lives more while spending less. How we feel going through life is what matters most, not what we have in material possessions.

BUDGETING YOUR MONEY

Now that we have earned it, protected it, and saved it, before we spend it, we should have a budget as our guide. Having a budget is a great way to keep the family from spending beyond their means. Virtually all of the families I work with say budgeting is important, and yet very few consistently follow one. When things get tight financially, suddenly budgeting comes front and center. As soon as things are no longer tight, they drift away from following a budget. This creates a family culture of spending whatever the family has.

The simplest way to think about a budget is to write down your total monthly income, or the money you will have to spend. Then list everything you need to spend money on monthly. This includes rent, utilities, food, entertainment, gas, clothing, cash spending limit, paying your kids for jobs outside their job for the family—everything. Then, total up this list of monthly expenses. Hopefully, it is less than your total income. If it is greater than your total income, you will need to adjust the budget until your total income can cover it. And don't forget to put "saving" as the first line item on your budget. I suggest starting with at least 5 percent and increasing it over time.

I like making budgeting a family team sport. Every family member can have one or more line items on the family budget they are responsible for, even as early as five or six years old. Here is how my sister and her four grandkids break it down in their household:

- Total income
  - Necessities:
  - Saving (5% minimum and 10% goal)
  - Home expenses
  - Food
  - Clothing
  - Kids' school expenses
  - Transportation expenses
  - Pet expenses
- Wants that can be cut if money becomes tight
  - Eating out
  - Vacations
  - Gifts
  - Entertainment
- Total money spent each month compared to total budgeted amount
- How much under or over budget
- Put any dollars left over from beating the budget into the family savings

This isn't a comprehensive list for my sister's family, but you get the idea. Every dollar they are under budget goes into additional savings. And the kids have a big say in how these additional savings can be used. This provides a strong motivation for them to actively participate in the family budgeting process.

The completed worksheet below will give you an idea of how to make this work for your own family.

MONTHLY HOUSEHOLD FORECAST

Monthly income $ __5,353__   Month __November__

Necessary (Needs) — Plan — Reality — Sponsor

Item	Plan	Reality	Sponsor
Savings	$ 500	$ 400	Parent 2
Housing	$ 1,800	$ 1,800	Parent 1
Transportation	$ 800	$ 800	Parent 1
Food/Groceries	$ 700	$ 650	Kid 1
Communication	$ 262	$ 262	Kid 2
	$	$	
	$	$	
	$	$	
Sub Total	$ 4,062	$ 3,912	

Extras (Wants)

Item	Plan	Reality	Sponsor
Personal Care	$ 165	$ 205	Parent 2
Streaming	$ 50	$ 50	Kid 1
Meals out	$ 240	$ 375	Parent 2
Clothing	$ 300	$ 267	Parent 2
Pets	$ 175	$ 180	Kid 1
Entertainment	$ 300	$ 305	Kid 2
	$	$	
	$	$	
	$	$	
Sub Total	$ 1,230	$ 1,382	
TOTAL	$ 5,292	$ 5,294	

Difference between budget and actual +/- $ __-2__

TOTAL SAVINGS Balance $ __24,514__

Dinner Table
© 2024 Dinner Table

Figure 3. Monthly Household Budget.

My desired outcome for having a budgeting process is to know exactly where I am with respect to money coming in and going out. And to track financial goals. It's not that hard to do as a family, especially if you make it a whole-family team sport! (Download a PDF of this exercise online.)

SPENDING YOUR MONEY

Now that you have a solid budget in place, how do you know you are getting the most value for your dollars when you spend it? The answer is whether or not we are wasting money or overpaying when it comes to spending money.

I suggest making this a family team sport as well. Look at all of the expenses on your family budget and ask, "Are we wasting or overpaying for each? Is there a better way to buy something that would save a significant amount of money for the family?"

On the waste side, once everyone in the family can see what it costs to pay the water bill, electric bill, food bill, and so on, they will be less likely to be wasteful. Hopefully, they will stop leaving the windows and doors open when the air conditioning is running. Or they may stop leaving the water running. Perhaps there are entertainment subscriptions or apps you've been paying for that no one is using anymore.

I love focusing on how you can buy better. My sister's family looked at how they were buying pet food and groceries. Rather than going to the grocery store each week, they started buying food in bulk. It was of better quality and overall about a 40 percent savings over what they had been spending. I enjoyed watching their excitement as they came up with these financial wins for the family.

Overpaying for things is something we all need to watch out for. Simple things like streaming services to watch the news, documentaries, and entertainment shows will creep up in cost over time. You may be surprised to find that you can watch the same shows on a different streaming service for a lot less. It's a good idea to check all subscriptions you are paying for at least once a year to see if you can get a better price, or if you need it anymore.

Bigger purchases like a vehicle, house, new furniture, and so on, need to be considered carefully as well. When I make a significant purchase, I always ask myself which option will give me the best long-term value. I have watched friends and family members purchase a less expensive car, thinking they were getting a good deal. And then the car would break down frequently, costing much more over time than if they had spent a little more up front for a car in better condition.

This same concept applies to home appliances, tools, and other items. Always ask: "What will the long-term cost be for making this purchase?" If you pay fifty percent more for an air conditioner that lasts twice as long and is more energy-efficient than the least expensive model, then paying 50 percent more upfront clearly saves you money in the long run. In my home budget, I have a line item to set aside money each month to account for the maintenance of larger items, which comes up every couple of years.

SHARING YOUR MONEY

Sharing money can feel really good, and at the same time, it might not always be helpful. As I mentioned previously, I have learned this the hard way over the years. When we share, we all want our contribution to help in some way. So how do you know if it will actually help?

Many times, the more money people believe we have, the more they request. This extends to investing in their companies. I've heard countless stories from friends who loaned or invested money in a friend's or family member's company, only to lose it all, despite being promised big returns.

We want to teach our kids to be generous by giving money and volunteering time to causes important to them. However, giving money doesn't mean it will always help. If your kids like animals, start by having them volunteer time at a shelter. If they are doing great work and making a difference, then sharing can extend to donating money to the shelter. When your kids share their time or money, a discussion about why they want to help and how they will know if it actually helps is powerful.

In my experience, most nonprofits are in business to make their payroll, more than to make a positive difference in the world, the way they claim. I always get involved first before giving, so I can see what is actually happening with money and other donated resources.

Around 2000, I visited Wolfsong Ranch, a wolf and wolf-dog rescue near Tucson, Arizona. They had about 150 animals on only ten acres. I wanted to get involved because I didn't want these animals to pay for the mistakes people make. Unfortunately, many states, counties, and cities outlaw all breeding of wolves and wolf-dogs. As a result, the cubs and pups would be euthanized unless a qualified rescue would take them.

I learned after volunteering at this rescue that they faced many challenges. I leaned in to get more involved, and I moved their location to southwestern New Mexico, facilitating the purchase of over six hundred acres. For four months straight, about thirty of my employees, friends, and I would drive down every weekend from Phoenix to build compounds. I stayed involved for about ten years. At our peak, we had over four hundred animals. My goal was to let these amazing animals live out their lives in carefully curated packs.

Had I just given money to Wolfsong Ranch, it would have gone mostly to waste. This is an example of making sure my sharing and giving really counted. In many ways, I feel like I rescued a rescue.

My desired outcome from sharing money and time is to make sure there is a net-positive difference in the world in a measurable, value-creation way. This goes for family members, friends, and causes.

INVESTING YOUR MONEY

What is your goal when investing money? Most people would say it is to get a good return on their investment. And when they do get a good return, they often spend all of what they made. I believe the goal of investing money is to first build a solid financial foundation for your family, and then responsibly grow it over time. This mindset is an important distinction. I like it because it clearly answers the question of why to invest, and from there, you can build your short-, medium-, and long-term financial goals.

Having a solid financial foundation means having enough liquid assets, or access to cash, to cover all of your expenses for a minimum number of months. And then grow from there. This minimum financial foundation will be whatever you are comfortable with.

Responsibly growing your family's financial foundation means continually growing it while not risking large amounts of it unnecessarily. You know you are doing this right when it is continually growing over time. It is important to have a financial investment strategy or plan that you stick to. This does not have to be complicated.

You can start this process with a goal of getting to three months of expenses in savings or other liquid investments. Once there, you can set a goal of increasing this by one month of additional monthly expenses in savings or liquid investments each year. You may grow at this pace for five years or so, and then increase it to two extra months of covered expenses each year.

As your investment accounts grow, as long as you continue to invest responsibly, you will see larger total dollar returns, allowing you to increase your nest egg even faster. I like setting a goal of not having to worry about income by a certain age. Personally, I don't believe the concept of retirement is a good idea. I think we need to stay in the game of creating value in the world for as long as we can. It keeps our brains sharp and emotional energy high. That said, maybe your investment goals target you not needing to work to support your family at fifty or sixty years old?

Every family can do this, no matter where you are starting from. You just need a plan and the discipline and patience to stick to it. And it's essential you do not live a lifestyle beyond your means. Living ten or twenty percent below your means is a good initial target that will allow you to build your family's financial nest egg faster.

Sometimes people come into a large amount of money that they have never experienced before. Large is relative to whatever a person's financial experience has been up to that point. Over the past ten years, I have had a number of acquaintances and friends come into a lot of money, usually from selling their business. These amounts range from a few million dollars to over one hundred million dollars. Each time, they asked me for advice on how to think about what to do with all this new money, since I have lived through it a few times.

My advice is always directionally the same. I suggest they do something nice to celebrate as a family, but that they don't change their lifestyle for at least twelve months. Instead, I encourage them to spend the year being a student of smart, responsible investing. And no matter what, don't invest in all of your friends' businesses or give large amounts away. It's no surprise that when people come into a lot of money that so many others line up to take it from you. I even suggest getting a T-shirt that has a big NO on the front. A good way to keep those vying for your money at bay is to say, "Per my strategy, I am not investing in anything for at least a year."

Very few heeded my advice and lost most or all of their new money in less than two years. Crazy! It is so hard for most of us to say "No" to family and friends. Unfortunately, there are manipulative people in the world who are good at convincing you to give them your money. A common trap is falling for what I call *circular unverified trust*.[IP] This is where others you know and trust have invested in something, so you think they did their homework, but they didn't. Always do your homework, due diligence before investing your money. Falling for *circular, unverified trust* has cost me millions over the years. I will never do this again.

With your kids, you can start early with small savings and build on it over time. As they get older, start discussing the purpose of investing to build their understanding and capability. Once they understand, it will be rewarding to watch their progress. Think about what this can do to add to the financial strength of the family. Not to mention the return on investment of your time by closing the bank of Mom and Dad for non-emergencies ten years earlier than most families these days.

Investment in your kids' education can pay big returns as long as it is the right education. Their education should be aligned with how they want to create value in the world. The goal isn't the diploma or degree. Companies pay for the value their team members can create, not a piece of paper. "The right education" can take many paths.

BORROWING MONEY

Borrowing money can be a useful tool when applied correctly. It can also get you into a lot of trouble fast if you are not careful. If you don't need to borrow money, then don't. If you always borrow responsibly, you will be fine. Responsible borrowing means the math makes sense for your family in that your family's financial foundation is not shrinking as a result. Any interest you are not paying on borrowed money is more money to put into growing your financial foundation.

Most families don't have enough cash to buy their first home. Borrowing money for a house at a good interest rate with payments well within your budget is a good investment over time. In this scenario, your home will appreciate over time, increasing your financial foundation. Sure, there are years where home values drop, but over time, like the stock market, they always bounce back, with a few exceptions.

Usually, people get into trouble when they are borrowing money to live above their means. This can be purchasing a more expensive house than they can afford. Buying a car they can't afford. Or just stacking up credit card debt by spending more than their monthly income will allow for.

Credit card companies and other lenders are in the business of loaning money. They are very good at convincing people to borrow money. You will have so much more money in the long run if you don't borrow to live above your means. I have seen borrowing build up in many families to where they are spending 25 percent or more of their monthly income paying the interest on their debt. When this happens, they are working for their credit card company and can be stuck doing so for years. No fun!

For businesses, borrowing money can be a very useful tool. In building my aerospace business, we would borrow money through a bank line of credit at a rate of around 4 percent. We would use that money to buy equipment and inventory to support our customers. Our average gross profit on each job was over 50 percent. So in simple math, we borrowed money at 4 percent to make a 50 percent profit on the work we did for our customers. Without borrowing money as a tool this way, we would not have been able to grow to one hundred million in sales as fast as we did. It requires cash to run and grow a business. And responsibly borrowing from a bank in this way is less expensive than raising cash by selling equity.

I hope this gave you some good ideas on how to think about each of these eight money skills. There are endless resources available for you to learn more about each skill. Having the right mindset and approach to setting financial goals is the first step. As you strengthen your ability in each of these skills, you can intentionally develop them in your kids and other family members. Consider developing a financial competency roadmap with your kids. Start with the basics when they are young and build on it over time, so they launch into adulthood being financially competent and independent if they so choose.

BIGGEST TAKEAWAYS FROM CHAPTER 4:

- Being financially competent is foundational to material value creation.
- Develop your list of the eight money skills in the order of importance that works best for your family.
- Build your family's financial foundation steadily and responsibly over time.
- Develop a financial competency roadmap for your kids
- Set a goal for when you want to close the bank of Mom and Dad for non-emergencies.

Chapter 5

TURN STRUGGLE INTO STRENGTH FOR YOUR FAMILY

Every Obstacle Contains an Opportunity

Have you noticed how most people complain when things get difficult? Rather than leaning into the struggle to improve their life condition, they act more like victims. I define struggle as any effort to strengthen a character trait, develop a capability, or improve one's life condition. It can be a micro-struggle or something much more intense.

All of the value is in the struggle. Think about some of the most successful adults you know, and I'll bet they had a fair amount of struggle when they were kids. And it is common to hear these same adults say they don't want their kids to struggle the way they did, so with the best of intentions, they often remove as much of this struggle as possible. My response is always, "Why would you deprive your kids of these healthy struggles that made you so amazing?"

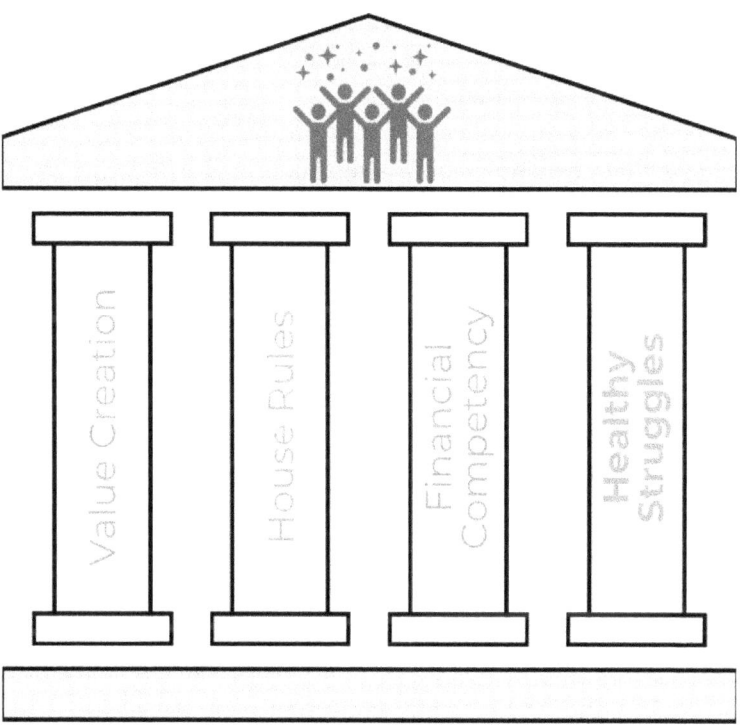

I don't see how any of us can improve without effort, and that equals struggle. If you could improve without effort, then the less you go to the gym, the stronger and more flexible you would become. It just doesn't work this way. Struggle can manifest in various forms: emotional, mental, or physical. It is important to regularly take our bodies, brains, and emotions to "the gym," so we continually strengthen all three. In time, your tolerance for struggle in each category will grow.

It's hard to increase your tolerance for struggle without first changing your relationship with it. If you believe all struggle is bad and run from it, then your tolerance will grow slowly, if at all. If you believe that all opportunities lie in the struggle, and that struggle is an essential component for growth, then you will quickly increase your tolerance the more you lean into creating value as a result of it.

The real value is keeping calm in the chaos. Staying calm allows you to handle more stressful things being thrown at you. It also prevents the same stressful things from continually repeating. This is the real secret to creating more value over time for your family. When we're stressed, it is harder to react to situations in a rational manner. This can damage relationships and make us miss opportunities, which is the opposite of creating value.

When we remove normal life struggles from our kids, we are not doing them any favors. In many cases, so much struggle is removed that by the time they are an adult at eighteen, they need another five to ten years (or more) to be ready for adulthood! I like to call these extra years the *emerging adult phase*.

I think about struggle in three major categories: healthy struggle, unhealthy struggle, and intentional struggle.

HEALTHY STRUGGLE

As a reminder, the touchstone for thinking about healthy struggles for your kids is in how they will develop the character, capabilities, and beliefs that will make them successful when they become adults. *Understanding* something is not the same as *being* something. My definition of "being" is the ability to apply a character trait, capability, or belief to create value in the world.

An example of this is having integrity. Your kids can *understand* that integrity means doing what you said you would do every time (even when no one is looking). But without the struggle of *embracing* this trait over time and truly seeing the value it creates in their lives, it won't develop into a strong trait. We see the result of not struggling to develop this trait all around us. I call it *situational integrity,* where someone only does what they said they would when it suits them.

There is no single strategy for developing kids to be successful adults. Nonetheless, there are categories required to be successful as an adult that seem to apply to all of us. People skills, interpersonal skills, communication skills, self-regulation skills, money skills, and a positive value-creation mindset are a few examples. Depriving our kids of normal, healthy struggles will stunt their development in some or all of these categories.

As your kids learn to navigate the social environment at school, they develop people, interpersonal, communication, and self-regulation skills.

Why is it important to develop these skills? Because kids must learn to create value.

Dealing with difficult kids is a normal, healthy struggle for developing these skills. Let's face it, many adults in the world are difficult to deal with, too, and we don't want our kids to be blindsided by such a situation when the time comes. Character, capabilities, and beliefs greatly impact all of these categories.

These days, so many kids adopt an entitlement mindset. Removing this mindset involves a healthy struggle. Look around. This struggle shows up the moment you start changing the rules and holding them more accountable and responsible.

That's why it's best to start adding accountability and responsibility early on, and gradually increase them until your kids are confident, capable, and self-reliant adults at eighteen. This is a normal and healthy struggle for your kids to go through. Let them figure it out, and learn and earn their way through it. Your job as a parent is to be a supportive and loving guide as they go through these struggles.

Another healthy struggle is rejection. Maybe your kid's sports team lost a game. Or maybe they weren't selected to be on their dream team. They can choose how to respond, like a victim or a victor. They can complain and make excuses, or they can mine the experience for learnings they can apply to get a better result next time.

A few other examples of healthy struggles for your kids might be:

- Getting homework consistently done on time
- Paying for more of their expenses as they get older
- Earning their own money
- Delaying gratification
- Developing people skills
- Building and strengthening relationships
- Managing time
- Choosing to be uncomfortable
- Discovering their passions

This list is not exhaustive; I am sure you can think of many more.

If you haven't already done so, make a conscious decision to feel good for your kids the next time they go through a healthy struggle. Rather than feeling bad for them, focus on the new skills they are developing within the struggle.

Ask yourself, what is the character trait, capability, or belief they are developing by experiencing this healthy struggle? Once this is identified, ask them questions that help them consider the positive outcomes. As always, this is a journey. It's about progress, not perfection or an expectation of instant learning and understanding.

UNHEALTHY STRUGGLE

Struggle does not equal trauma. Trauma refers to a deeply distressing or overwhelming experience that significantly impacts a person's mental, emotional, and physical well-being. It can be caused by a single event or prolonged exposure to stressful or dangerous situations. How you respond to trauma goes a long way toward its impact on your life.

Unhealthy struggle is something you wouldn't intentionally want anyone to go through, but life happens, and we have to deal with it. Unhealthy struggles come in many forms, such as addiction, divorce, injury, death in the family, serious illness, physical abuse, and more.

When an unhealthy struggle comes upon us with little to no warning, we can deal with it in one of two ways. We can dwell on it, develop a victim mindset, and stay stuck for much longer than necessary. Or we can do all we can to improve our life condition, discover what we learned from the struggle, and apply those learnings to create even more value in the future.

Most of us are pretty good at coaching people going through unhealthy struggles, pointing out productive ways to get through them. It's important to talk to yourself when going through unhealthy struggles in the same way. The challenge is that what we intellectually understand about going through a significant struggle will feel much more intense emotionally. When it happens to you, keep going back to how you would advise someone you care about if they were in the same situation.

I have had a few unhealthy struggles in my life so far, and I'm sure there will be more. It happens to all of us. One was a serious staph infection at the beginning of my sophomore year in high school. I came in for dinner one evening, complaining about a pain in my groin that was getting worse. I also had red streaks running up my left leg from my toe that I had cut a couple of days earlier. When I showed my mom, she said it was just a rash and not to worry about it. I woke up at two a.m. that night, screaming in pain, and my leg had literally doubled in diameter.

My parents didn't want to take me to the hospital because of what it would cost, so we argued for a while until I convinced them to take me. I told them that I would pay them back whatever it cost. I spent two nights in the hospital, where the doctors were deciding if the best option to save my life was to amputate. I did not like this idea, and my emotions around the thought of it were intense!

The human body is an amazing thing. The swelling stopped right at my groin, and the doctors didn't understand how the infection didn't spread to the rest of my body. There were several spots on my leg that were dark with what looked like bruising, and one of them popped. The pressure it relieved gave me a few minutes of less than excruciating pain. The doctors said this was a sign of the body healing, and they would watch and wait before making a decision to amputate my left leg.

The recovery process was brutal. I spent months in bed with incredible pain. I would soak every day in an antibiotic soap with about a dozen open wounds on my leg, constantly oozing. When my friends would come over, I would ask them, with hope in my voice, "It's looking better, right?" Their faces would almost always turn white after looking at my leg. The doctors told me I would never walk right again, and it took over a decade for the infection to completely go away. I took powerful antibiotics each time the infection would flare up. Thankfully, these flare-ups grew further and further apart until they finally stopped years later.

So what did I learn that I could apply to create more value in the future? I learned how to be my own health advocate. I learned pain tolerance. I learned how serious infections can be and the best way, on a budget, to treat my condition. I learned discipline and extreme patience in my physical therapy to recover full function in my leg. I even learned to wiggle each toe independently from the others to take my mind off the pain!

Fast forward: despite what the doctors had told me, I went on to run over a dozen marathons and three ultramarathons, complete three Ironman competitions, and earn my sixth-degree black belt in ITF Taekwon-Do. This included doing demonstration-breaking at tournaments where I would jump, do the splits mid-air, and break boards on each side. I have had a total of six surgeries on my left leg, but I was determined not to let the infection win or let what the doctors predicted come true.

When I tell my physician friends about this experience, they all have a similar response. Most people never fully recover from such injuries because they are not willing to consistently put in the work for the years recovery takes. I still have to do daily physical therapy to keep my leg high-functioning. If I let up even for a week, I can feel the decline starting. Actually, what a great motivator to work out every day!

The benefits from this unhealthy struggle have helped me and others in many ways. In 2010, I believe that being my own health advocate saved my life. I had internal bleeding. My body required fifteen units of blood via transfusion before the bleeding stopped. I was in the hospital with a nurse practitioner friend, telling me I should do what the doctors were telling me. Instinctively, I knew they were wrong, so I called a physician friend at the Mayo Clinic for advice. He said to get over to Mayo as fast as possible, or one of two tragic outcomes would take place. According to him, I would likely die or, at a minimum, have a heart attack.

I appreciated his candor.

I immediately called three other friends: one to get me a helicopter, one to get me released from the hospital, and another to take care of the paperwork to get admitted into Mayo. Within fifteen minutes, the helicopter landed on the helipad outside my window in the ICU. Interestingly, the hospital I was in did not want me to leave; they were worried about their liability. Had it taken longer than an additional five minutes, I would have ripped out my IVs and crawled to the helicopter. And during all of this, my blood pressure was forty-eight over eighteen. I had to keep my feet elevated just to prevent passing out.

Thankfully, it all worked out, and my physician friend at Mayo said he believed the only reason I pulled through was from being in excellent physical condition. It makes me wonder, had I not struggled with the leg infection and proving those doctors wrong, I might not have maintained physical fitness. Or I might have simply accepted the advice from those doctors and stayed at that hospital. If so, I might have bled out and died, and you wouldn't be reading this book.

My experience with this early example of an unhealthy struggle has allowed me to help many others going through similar struggles. One of the biggest lessons it taught me was to never give up.

Think about your family. Which path will you choose when an unhealthy struggle is upon you or your family members? How will you support and coach your kids the next time they encounter an unhealthy struggle?

INTENTIONAL STRUGGLE

Intentional struggle is about developing character and capabilities and removing limiting beliefs through purposeful design. As you go through and refine this exercise with your kids about how they want to show up as adults, start designing healthy struggles with them. Ultimately, your kids will have to own how they show up as an adult someday. The sooner they can accept developmental struggles along the way as their idea, the better.

In the Note to the Reader section, I mentioned the *Value Creation Cycle*[IP]. I didn't know what to call it when I was six, but I experienced it nonetheless. I would struggle to develop a capability I could use to earn money; it built my confidence, and I applied the new capability to create value for customers, ultimately earning more money. See Figure 4 below.

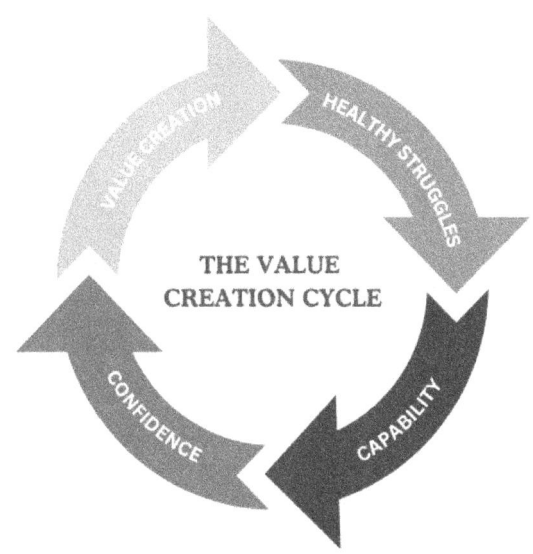

Figure 4. The Value Creation Cycle.

I kept repeating this cycle over and over again as a kid, and I am still doing it today. The capabilities I developed to earn money early on allowed me to live on my own and be fully financially self-reliant at seventeen. Living the Value Creation Cycle continually modifies my limiting beliefs about what is and is not possible; after completing each cycle, I learn that I can do anything I am willing to put the effort into.

I learned to trust and value the struggle, knowing I would always emerge stronger on the other side if I continued doing the hard and smart work. This allows me to take on more and more difficult struggles as my tolerance for them increases.

Your kids are mature enough to talk about Intentional Struggle. We've found a natural way to start this conversation.

1. Ask them about their personal goals.
2. Invite them to share about how they want to show up as an adult someday.
3. Discuss how character traits, capabilities, and beliefs come into play for each goal.

For example, if a twelve-year-old child says they want to start and operate a business someday because they love watching Mom run her business, here is a potential plan.

Goal: Run my own business someday as an adult (maybe sooner)

Character required:

- Integrity
- Perseverance
- Passion
- Positive energy
- Fairness and can make tough decisions

Capabilities required:

- Assessing business ideas
- Preparing a business plan
- Understanding financial statements and budgeting
- Hiring talent (eventually)
- Having great customer service skills

Beliefs required:

- I can do this.
- There is always a better way, and it is my job to find it.
- All the value is in the struggle.
- Business is a team sport.
- I love working with people.

You don't need a comprehensive list for every goal your kids have, but you get the idea. For each goal, what work will they have to put into it to be successful in achieving it? If your kid wants to make the track team, they will need to be competitive.

- How much time will they have to put into training (building capability)?
- What amount of mental toughness will they need to keep going and handle rejection along the way (character traits)?
- What negative thoughts will they need to overcome (modifying limiting beliefs)?

Living the *value-creation cycle* has made for quite the journey so far. The stress of growing up in a low-income household created a struggle that forced me to build character, capabilities, and even overcome self-limiting beliefs. The money I could earn outside the family and friends circles kept growing as I continued going around the *value-creation cycle*. It grew to the point that, by the time I was twenty years old, I didn't worry at all about sustaining my lifestyle financially.

In my early twenties, I formed a band with a wonderful woman, an amazing singer, and a single Mom with two kids. We soon moved in together, and I did my part in supporting what I considered my new family. I worked full-time during the day, and the band was a business we shared in the evenings and weekends. In the first half of the 1980s, we performed over a thousand shows together. Debye has since passed from her battle with cancer, and I am still very close to her son and his family. They are family to me.

It wasn't until the early 1990s that I started my first business. Leaning into the healthy struggle of starting and building businesses has led to eight businesses so far, and I am invested in many others. I couldn't have imagined, when I started my first business, that I would have come this far or been able to handle some of the crazy, intense struggles along the way. But that is the magic of the value-creation cycle. It makes you grow the value you can create in a way that picks up speed the more you follow it.

Who knows, your kids may be excited about embracing struggle. If not, I hope this chapter has given you some ideas on how to start a conversation with them about the value of struggle and changing their relationship with it.

BIGGEST TAKEAWAYS FROM CHAPTER 5:

- Three categories of struggle: healthy, unhealthy, and intentional
- Let your kids struggle more in order to develop the character, capabilities, and beliefs that will make them successful value-creating adults
- Apply learnings from unhealthy struggles to become stronger and create even more value in the world
- Value-creation cycle: Struggle to develop a capability, build confidence, and use the new capability to create value. Then, repeat the cycle while taking even bigger steps
- Your kids will be more motivated when they own their goals

Chapter 6

DON'T SETTLE FOR GOING SOLO

Tap into Deeper Family Wisdom

According to a poll by the American Psychiatric Association in February 2025, one in three Americans experiences loneliness at least once a week.[1] And while technology can help maintain relationships, it can also be a double-edged sword, contributing to loneliness. It is well documented that loneliness contributes to declining physical health, mental health, and longevity. In short, drifting away from meaningful connections with family and communities is hazardous to your health—literally.

We have a crisis of community. Families are less and less part of strong, healthy communities that watch out for each other and have "each other's backs." You don't have to go it alone, and if you are, it is by choice. Being part of a healthy

---

[1] "Media Advisory: New Polling Data on Loneliness, Experts Available from American Psychiatric Association." American Psychiatric Association. February 26, 2025. https://www.psychiatry.org/news-room/news-releases/media-advisory-new-polling-data-on-loneliness-expe.

community of families offers a deep resource for practical family wisdom. You can use this wisdom to create more value for your family. And your family wisdom, developed over the years, can help many other families create additional value and more effectively navigate challenging times.

It can be uncomfortable sharing too much information about your family. Who wants to share financial challenges, frustrations, fears, marital stress, bad behavior, and other sensitive topics? At the same time, wouldn't it be nice to have a trusted community of families as a sounding board or resource, along with getting their advice on how they successfully navigated these challenges?

Sharing sensitive family topics outside the family isn't a muscle most people exercise. We live in a culture where everyone seems to be an expert on what is wrong with people and the world. No one likes being unfairly judged. As a result, many people and families present a picture they want the world outside their family to see. And so they stay in a silo when it comes to more effectively creating value as a family.

Receiving help requires trust that has to be earned. You can't just tell a community of families to please start sharing and helping each other, and have it magically happen. Families are in different places when it comes to their ability to even see what needs to be worked on regarding their family value-creation journey. That said, there are

THE FOUNDATION FOR ALL THE VALUE BEING CREATED IN THE WORLD STARTS WITH THE FAMILY.

common topics of conversation that over 90 percent of families are interested in having. These conversations are where trust starts to build, and as a result of opening up and sharing, it's also where receiving help begins.

The foundation for all the value being created in the world starts with the family. Families are raising kids to be amazing adults, and they should own that responsibility, not turn it over to influences outside the family that usually have conflicting interests. What has a better chance of influencing your kids to show up as amazing humans now and when they become adults? Is it character, behaviors, and beliefs developed within your family? Or is it outside influences with often-conflicting interests found within our education system, social media, politics, and peers?

Having the right conversations and building trust is key.

One community of families I've been working with for just over a year in Phoenix, Arizona, is proving this. Once a month, we meet on a Saturday for conversations around a family value-creation topic. The sessions last about two hours. These are facilitated discussions, not presentations or preaching in any way. I set up the topic, ask a few questions to check for levels of understanding, and then we do some work for each family represented in the room. Each family takes a few minutes to answer some questions. Then, small groups of families share what they learned or discovered. And this is followed by sharing the biggest takeaways from each table for the entire group to hear and benefit from.

When discussing the monthly themed topics, families begin to open up and share challenges and areas where they want to create more value as a family. Within several communities I lead, this trust starts to develop quickly. Usually, within two to three meetings. The community of families I facilitate in Phoenix started with four families and now has over fifty families, thirteen months later. And this growth has been purely from word of mouth.

I have developed a twelve-month cycle of topics designed to be evergreen, so you can revisit them every year for decades and still derive more value each time your family goes through them. One way to think about this is that businesses create value as they evolve from a start-up to small, medium, and eventually large businesses, if they do things right. Throughout this entire evolution, they talk about marketing every year. The businesses that succeed are those that continually improve their marketing each year, among many other things. The same holds true for your family when it comes to the foundational ways your family can create value.

Figure 5 below illustrates twelve months of deep-dive conversation topics with communities of families.

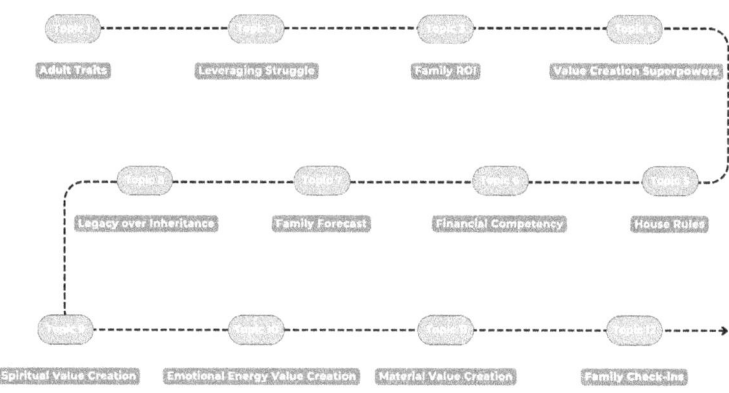

Figure 5. Deep-dive family conversation topics.

A touchstone in all of these conversations is the Dinner Table Method and Value Creation Cycle. It's helpful to check in on how families are talking about and taking action on creating value, house rules, financial competency, and leveraging struggle. I recommend looking back three or six months and asking, "Are we creating more value as a family today than we were then?" If you are, then you are on the right track. If not, work together as a family and with your community of families to adjust your approach. There is always a better way to create value than you can think of today, and it is your job to find it! This mindset contributes significantly to personal growth.

With the communities I facilitate and lead, new members are coming in all the time. Each deep dive topic is designed to be stand-alone and create a lot of value for every family, even if it is their first session. There is no beginning or end to the order, just evergreen family value creation. No matter when a family starts in the community, the common theme is preparing your kids to launch into adulthood and creating value more effectively for each family present.

Conversations with your kids about who they want to be when they become adults, centered on the topics of character, capabilities, and beliefs, have been transformational. I call them Ready to Launch Conversations[IP]. It's one thing to look at a well-put-together list in all three categories and want it all. When presented with a list of value-creating character traits, capabilities, and beliefs, most family members have a hard time deciding which will be the most beneficial. I have never known anyone to master everything in one lifetime, so you must choose what to focus on. There is a healthy struggle in choosing, doing the required work, and refining the right list for your family and each family member.

Each time we talk about leveraging struggle, I'm surprised by how few families see the value in it. Initially, without the framework of a healthy struggle, any real struggle is seen as bad. Yet for a few people in the group, some of the struggles discussed aren't seen as "real struggles." In a recent session, one family was talking about the struggle of getting their kids to consistently do their homework and help around the house. A father at another table was shaking his head, saying that isn't real struggle. When I asked what he meant, he said not having enough money to make rent that month was a real struggle. The truth is, both are real struggles with different ramifications if not resolved.

I love it when families voice different versions of struggle in each community session. It helps with improving perspective and makes getting through any struggle seem more possible. When the struggle of needing to earn more money for the family came up, we discussed what it would take to earn just 10 percent more money in the next year. With the input of the community members, it seemed more possible than before the session.

If you make a 10 percent improvement each year for seven years, you will have nearly doubled your income. My experience says if you focus on this goal and do the hard and smart work to achieve it, the increase in income accelerates more than 10 percent as the years go on. I have had my income increase more than tenfold in some years. But I have been working on increasing it for forty-five years so far. My early years were more in the ten percent range.

Exploring what the return on investment (ROI) will be for your family to do this work is eye-opening. A great question is, "At what age does the bank of Mom and Dad close for non-emergency things?" Usually, I hear a roar of laughter when I ask this.

If we are laying the groundwork to consistently create holistic value as a family, what will be the long-term benefits? Money is always a big topic. The more financially competent and responsible kids are, the stronger the family's financial foundation will be, now and when they become adults.

Intentionally asking kids to improve what it feels like to be part of the family is having a significant ROI impact, according to the families. It seems obvious that family members should do this naturally, but making it part of everyone's job for the family keeps it front and center. This drives the emotional and connectedness value creation within families.

Helping your kids discover their value creation superpowers is always a fun conversation. All kids gravitate toward something. Start there. In a recent session, one young man of fourteen said he didn't have anything. However, I noticed he always had different types of Rubik's Cubes with him. His mom chimed in, saying he loves solving problems. The discussion turned to how valuable problem-solvers are within organizations. This was his superpower to continue cultivating! Or, at least, one of them. His demeanor changed in the following sessions, showing more confidence and value in himself.

Establishing structure within families can be challenging. Even when it is discussed and agreed to, consistently following a structure is complex. Regularly touching base as a community on setting family goals and expectations, earning money, and expenses your kids pick up truly helps. This topic always brings out amazing wisdom on how to do this well, which helps families address challenges they are experiencing. All of this is a work in progress for each family, and a little struggle here will pay huge dividends down the road.

Financial competency is often a challenging conversation in groups due to how emotionally charged the topic of money is for many families. The more our families discuss the topic as a group, the more they see money as nothing more than a tool, and they continually modify their limiting beliefs around money. Like many things, money is not all or nothing. You have to start somewhere and build from there. It took me twenty-three years to build a company from zero to one worth well into nine figures. And it took me twenty-three years of healthy struggle before I was ready to start that company.

Improving your family's ability to create material value—money—has much to do with mindset. Two words that frequently come up in our group sessions are "entitlement" and "earned." Many kids and adults just want what they want now, without having to put in the work. One young man said he wanted to be where I am in terms of career and financial status. I responded by saying, "Don't you mean earn where I am currently at?" If you start earning money with a value-creation mindset, there is no end to how much you can earn if that is important to you. Remember, money is just part of creating value holistically.

Family financial forecasting is about setting goals as a family and trying to achieve them as a team sport. It's about who owns what item on the family budget and how you celebrate when you win. With newer families to the community, I often see expressions of disbelief when I discuss making family budgeting and forecasting a whole family exercise. Many parents will say their kids do not need to see the family's finances. They do not want them to worry about this; they want them to focus on school. I say this is another healthy struggle we are not exposing many kids to, which is not helping them prepare for adulthood.

Many families share stories about how goal-setting and budgeting become a family team sport and a lot of fun. There are always creative ways to save and spend money more wisely. With all family members' brains in the game, I have yet to hear one family say it didn't improve their finances.

> **INHERITANCE IS ABOUT DIVIDING AND HOPING FOR THE BEST.**

I see a big distinction between legacy and inheritance. Legacy is about building over time, including from one generation to the next. Inheritance is about dividing and hoping for the best. In my experience, giving unearned money in any form usually doesn't work out for the best. Simply stated, if you didn't earn it, you probably won't be good at managing it. Think of all the stories you have heard of lottery winners losing it all within a short period of time.

I get it. The parents did well, and when they passed on, the kids were sometimes waiting impatiently for "their" money. This is an entitlement mindset. I have witnessed many family squabbles over what siblings believed to be an unfair distribution from a family member's will. I have seen equal entitlement passion here vying for amounts ranging from a few thousand dollars to tens of millions or more. It's all relative to what someone considers as a lot of money and how they view entitlement and fairness.

A legacy mindset makes a family stronger than having an entitlement mindset. This presents as a family intentionally building material, emotional, and spiritual value in the current generation and developing kids to contribute to growing the value in all three categories in the next generation as it is passed on.

A common thing I hear is, "We don't have a lot of money, so it doesn't matter." I remind them that I started financially in the negative when my parents racked up debt in my name after kicking me out of the house in high school. From there, I built multi-generational wealth. You have to start somewhere. But you still have to start. This is my forty-six-year overnight success story since being kicked out of the house. It really makes community members think when I ask what they believe is possible for them if they were to put in the right effort for forty-six years.

Discussing spiritual value creation requires us to quickly clear up a few things to have a productive conversation. Some interpret using the word *spiritual* to mean religion. Half of those in the room are deeply religious and immediately think this is what spiritual value creation means. The other half may be offended because they do not want religion pushed on them. When I explain that spiritual value creation is about connectedness at its core, everyone engages in a positive discussion.

Connectedness starts with the family and spreads out from there. Community, causes, God, wherever each family and family member chooses to take it. I love what it feels like to interact with each of the communities I have the pleasure and honor of facilitating and leading. I always make it a point to tell them this and describe the impact of our strengthening connections. Seeing new friendships being formed between kids and parents is rewarding. Watching them lean in to help one another solve significant challenges in a caring and supportive way is what being part of a healthy community is all about. Being there for each other without hidden agendas.

I went to a piano recital that one of the grandmothers in a community was putting on for her students. Close to half the families in the room were connected to my community. It was such a warm feeling with so many coming up to give me a hug and wanting to chat. I imagined the loss I'd feel if I were not connected to this community. This piano teacher and I are now in conversations to play a show together, her on piano and me on guitar. I can't wait!

Leading discussions on emotional energy value creation is one of my favorite conversations to have. It's so valuable and yet few families engage in conversations on this topic. Families report that being aware of how each family member impacts the whole creates a new, positive effect. Many families create job descriptions where each member is responsible for elevating healthy, positive emotional energy. As I mentioned earlier, positive emotional energy is the scarcest commodity on the planet to me because it supercharges everything we do. Looking at positive emotional energy as a form of value that a family creates is a different way of thinking. I like to ask, "Who owns what when it comes to creating value for your family?"

Eventually, each family member will have the responsibility of creating value in all three categories (material, emotional, spiritual). And some have more responsibility in one category than the others.

As you might imagine, material value (money) is a front-and-center topic for most of the families I work with in low-income communities. But I also find that families at every income level often have issues with money. Way too many families are living on the edge of what they earn. The community discussions center around what it would feel like to be financially secure. And from there, what it will take to make that happen.

I like to start with how families are spending money now. They can always find ways to earn more money over time, but they need help now. It's good to be working on both at the same time. Figure out how to live below your means now, while developing the capability to earn more money in the future. Most parents are afraid, if not terrified, to talk openly in a group about money. The fear eases with community support and taking small steps in each category. Being intentional here is key as well. Sitting back and hoping things will change is never a good strategy.

When I said at the beginning of this chapter, "If you are going it alone by not having a community of families to lean on, it is by choice," I meant it. We can all identify other families to draw strength from and create value more effectively as a family and as a growing community. Start by identifying one family you share values with. This chapter and book give you a framework for discussions if you choose to meet monthly or quarterly. I prefer monthly meetings that last about two hours. If you tag on breakfast or a barbecue, even better!

When building your community, consider the values the families you have identified to be part of your community have, and the values of the friends your kids have. I highly recommend having this discussion as a family. For your kids, take what you came up with for character traits, capabilities, and behaviors they would like to have when they become adults. Now consider which of their friends will help them move in this direction and which are going down a different path. We are significantly influenced by who we hang out with the most.

BIGGEST TAKEAWAYS FROM CHAPTER 6:

- Loneliness is a real problem affecting one in three Americans and growing
- Most families create value in silos
- Make time for meaningful family value-creation discussions with other families
- Build your own community of families with shared values
- Help your kids cultivate circles of friends that will support them in how they want to show up as an adult one day

Chapter 7

LEAD CLEARLY AND BOLDLY

Every Family Member Has an Influential Role

Most families have one matriarch or patriarch who provides the primary leadership for their family. This influence can often spread across multiple generations. This makes sense as it is natural for all of us to align behind and follow strong, capable, and moral leaders. Most of the time, this happens naturally within families and without much intentionality.

GRANDMA GREAT

A childhood friend of mine invited me to his wedding on the coast of Washington State in 1995. It was held at a beautiful beachfront property that had been in their family since the 1940s. There were lots of family members attending, representing four generations. On my first lap around the property, I met an elderly woman with amazing energy. I found out she was my friend's grandmother. Her name was Inga, and her family referred to her as Grandma Great. Inga was one of twelve children (three girls and nine boys) and ninety-two years old when I met her.

Grandma Great pulled me aside and wanted to know all about how I knew her grandson, Rob. She asked me when and where we met. Then she went deeper with her questions. She asked what our common interests were in 1975 and what they were on the day we chatted back in 1995. She asked how often we get to see each other now that we live four states apart. Then she shifted to wanting to know all about me. I never encountered someone who was so interested in asking me questions about myself.

The next morning, she had one of the family members come and get me. When I arrived, she made me eggs for breakfast, and we had another thoughtful conversation, but this time about the future. She asked me to commit to always being there for her grandson if he ever needed it. Of course, I replied. It was an unspoken commitment I had made with myself anyway. Rob is like family to me and always will be. I love him like a brother.

I was struck by how intentional Grandma Great was in our conversations and by her leadership in setting the stage for her generations of family members to thrive after she passes one day. Making me breakfast that weekend may seem like a small thing, but I remember several family members being surprised, saying that she never does that for anyone she has just met. She saw something in me, and I will never forget what it felt like to be with her thirty years ago.

After that weekend, I asked my friend about his grandmother. He said she is and has always been the strength holding the family together. Grandma Great was a nurse before retirement and deeply cared about people. She was clearly the matriarch, and it was easy to see why from my two conversations with her and watching her interact with the family. This was the first time I really began to consider family leadership. Grandma Great passed away in 2002 at the age of ninety-nine.

What makes these family leaders different, and how do they show up for their families? I have interviewed a number of individuals providing strong leadership for their families as they lead by example. From the outside, they appear to provide strong leadership in the community and for their families.

When I ask who was, or is, the strong patriarch or matriarch they looked to when growing up, they all had one. There were a few common ways these family leaders were described. They told family members they could be whatever they wanted to be, and encouraged them to pursue their dreams and chosen path. They had tremendous wisdom and helped immensely with difficult decisions. And they provided a safety net of emotional strength.

Although all the individuals I interviewed said their family matriarch or patriarch provided strong leadership, not once did I discover a list of what it meant to be a strong leader within any of these families. A few families intentionally get their kids ready to go into the family business, and hopefully, take it over someday. Leadership was part of the conversation to go into the family business, but they did nothing that would intentionally get them ready to lead or be a leader within the family. In my research, the matriarchs and patriarchs mostly led by example and did not follow an intentional leadership trait list of what it means to be a leader within their families.

The definition of leadership that makes the most sense to me is *creating value with and through others*. This applies to business as well as family. Businesses that intentionally cultivate and develop their leadership capability perform significantly better than those that don't. What would be different for your family if you intentionally cultivated your kids to be leaders within the family?

Few businesses do a good job of intentionally developing their leaders to be capable and moral leaders. As a result, in my experience working with thousands of leaders, only about 10 percent of leaders develop into strong, capable, and moral leaders. Moral leaders create positive value in the world. Leaders who lack morality in their decision-making more often than not take value out of the world solely for their benefit. Capable and moral leaders create value for all stakeholders involved.

If you asked your family members what it means to be a leader in the family, what would they say? We all recognize strong, capable, and moral leadership when we see it. Most of us can describe it and appreciate it when we experience this type of leadership. It feels good when we are exposed to it. Rather than just letting it pass as a good or amazing experience, the challenge is to write it down, refine it over time, and live it. Yes, it does take some work. But the rewards can be exponential.

> **MORAL LEADERS CREATE POSITIVE VALUE IN THE WORLD. LEADERS WHO LACK MORALITY IN THEIR DECISION-MAKING MORE OFTEN THAN NOT TAKE VALUE OUT OF THE WORLD SOLELY FOR THEIR BENEFIT.**

I asked one of my grandnieces, when she turned sixteen, what it means to be a leader in the family. Admitting she had never been asked that question before, here is the list she gave me in just a few minutes:

- Good problem-solver
- Safe space to talk
- Model healthy behavior
- Model healthy character traits

- Encourage the development of each family member
- Provide structure and accountability, set house rules
- Encouraging and planning more family time together to strengthen relationships
- Grow the family balance sheet:
    - Money (material value)
    - Energy (emotional value)
    - Connectedness (spiritual value)

I encourage you to come up with your own list of what it means to be a leader within your family. You will surely refine and strengthen it over time if you intentionally develop all family members to move in that direction. There is no one way or perfection here. It is all about creating value as a family and continually getting better at it over time.

And as always, enjoy the journey because that is truly the only thing any of us have. As I have previously stated, if you are creating more value as a family today than you were six months or a year ago, then you are heading in the right direction. Celebrate it and build on it!

As you are developing and strengthening what it means to be a leader within your family, here are a few categories to consider:

- How family members show up as leaders
- Activities that create the most value for your family
- Communities of families and circles of friends
- Family balance sheet: material (money), emotional (energy), spiritual (connectedness)

HOW FAMILY MEMBERS SHOW UP AS LEADERS

The strongest family leaders I know always seem to have a plan for the family's future. No matter what is going on in the world, they are building momentum for the family and not waiting for the world to do it for them. They maintain positive emotional energy in tough times, tackling challenges as they come. They are consistent in how they show up, which fosters a lot of trust. They don't complain, just take action. They care deeply, even when tough love is required. They are present and make time for every family member. In short, they carry the weight of the family's well-being, fulfillment, and happiness with strength and emotional maturity.

Strong family leaders also make time to care for themselves, so they have the energy to always be there for the family. They are always learning, growing, and leading by example. They never seem to stay stuck in fixed ways of thinking; they chip away at limiting beliefs. There is always a better way than they can think of today, and they are continually looking for it. They are inspiring to watch and be around, and never make it solely about themselves. Being successful as a whole is always the most important thing to the family.

Some family members seem to naturally have what it takes to be a strong leader. Most don't show up that way, but does it mean they can't? A question I have heard a lot over the years is, "Are leaders born or built?" If you go by my definition of leadership, that leadership is creating value with and through others. Then we are all leaders, and we are all on the path of being "built" into better leaders. It's a choice and a responsibility we all must make. So the question becomes, do you want to increase your leadership capability a notch and create even more value? There is no limit to how far you can take this in one lifetime.

Most kids I work with don't believe being a leader is in the cards for them when initially discussed. When I give them my definition of leadership and say yes, they can be a leader, their eyes almost always light up with possibilities.

My grandniece and I were discussing applying for her first job. She had a list of companies she wanted to apply to, including fast food, clothing, hotel, and others. I asked why she thought these businesses hire employees for entry-level positions, or any position at all. Her reply was to work with customers and basically do the job they would ask her to do.

This grandniece is fully managing the household budget; it was a bit of a healthy struggle for her to get there, but she did. I mentioned that when she manages the household budget, the goal is to stay within the budget and preferably beat it and have even more money than planned left over. She smiled and said yes, we have been beating the budget for over five months in a row.

I told her that running a business is no different than your household budget. You have money coming in from customers, or total revenue. Then you have all the expenses (costs) to run the business. And finally, what is left over is profit. When they hire you, you are joining a team to help them create as much value as possible while always having satisfied customers. In other words, you are being hired to help them create value measured in satisfied customers and profit.

If, when you interview, you understand this, you will have a big advantage over other applicants. How many hiring managers hear from an applicant, "I am here to interview for this position, and if you hire me, help you create as much value as I can for your business. Please let me know where to start and the best way to do this." I think most hiring managers would fall out of their chairs!

The first step is telling your kids they can be leaders in the family and they can create value in the world. And it is important to describe what that looks like, both within the family and in the world, on their journey to adulthood and beyond. Here is a partial list of what I model to be a leader within my family:

- Fulfill my agreed-upon job for the family and encourage accountability for other family members to do theirs
- Intentionally develop all family members to create more value over time at their own pace and on their chosen journey
- Model and encourage healthy struggle
- Be a safe sounding board for any challenge that comes up, no matter how uncomfortable
- Be consistent and fair
- Lead growing the holistic family balance sheet as a team sport, materially, emotionally, and spiritually
- Character traits:
    - Patience
    - Integrity
    - Grit (perseverance)
    - Empathy
    - Productive positivity (Optimist and Realist in approach to creating value)

Again, there is no one-size-fits-all. And if you want to intentionally develop your kids to be family leaders, and even hone your own leadership skills as a parent, it is helpful to define it as a family. Then refine it over time as your family starts and continues intentionally living it. No one gets this right on the first draft.

ACTIVITIES THAT CREATE THE MOST VALUE FOR YOUR FAMILY

Every family is a little different when it comes to their lifestyle and schedules. Spending time together is common across most families. How your family spends that time can really make a difference. Every minute together is an opportunity to strengthen connections and develop your kids.

Dinner table discussions without electronic devices is an excellent opportunity to check in as a family and keep building value. I like having family members take turns leading dinner table discussions on a topic that is interesting or important to them. To help promote positive emotional energy when the world seems to dwell at times on what is wrong with everything, ask each family member to describe the best part of their day. My goal is to guide dinner table discussions to be fun and energizing, while strengthening the family.

Once a month, I gather the family to discuss our family goals and what it means to be a leader within the family. This is always about my family members talking much more than I do, especially the kids. We continually refine our goals, which are moving targets as we accomplish more. Within this process, I naturally see the self-limiting beliefs fade. Family leadership is refined a lot in the first few months, then settles into a solid list. In the beginning of these conversations, family leadership feels abstract, but over time, it crystallizes into a solid list. Our monthly discussions on leadership mature into conversations around how we are living these leadership qualities and enjoying the benefits they produce.

I also like to take one to two hours a month with each kid and review their list of how they want to show up when they become an adult someday. We unpack their personal goals and their list of character traits, capabilities, and beliefs. We keep a running list of their interests as well. This isn't lecture time for me. It's more of a conversation of, "What do you think, what would you like to do and why, and if you do that, what will happen next?" It is so fulfilling to watch them develop through these conversations on their journey to becoming amazing value-creating adults. It also strengthens our connection and deepens my love for each of them.

One of the biggest surprises for me was how families resonate with running the family budget as a team sport. It's such a solid capability the kids develop, and it has and continues to strengthen my family unit. The kids love having a say in how the excess money is spent when they beat the monthly budget.

Another activity I like is having regular half-day check-ins with each kid, with no agenda. I do this once a quarter and leave it up to each kid what we do. In all of these activities, I nudge the family members to keep going in the direction of creating more value over time. And by value, I mean the right balance of material, emotional, and spiritual value.

Everyone has a job for the family they agreed to do. We all depend on each other to do their job so we can thrive as a family. This builds a sense of purpose and appreciation within our kids.

COMMUNITIES OF FAMILIES AND CIRCLES OF FRIENDS

Who do your kids hang out with the most? Who we invest time with today is a good predictor of who we will become in the future because of their influence. And it's not just their close circle of friends, it's the internet, podcasts, social media, games, influencers, YouTube channels, and more.

As a family leader, you can help guide your kids to be more intentional here as well. Now that you and your kids have a refined list of the character traits, capabilities, and beliefs that will make them the most successful now and when they become adults someday, what are the ideal qualities their circle of friends should have that will support this list? Figure 6 is an example of what this can look like:

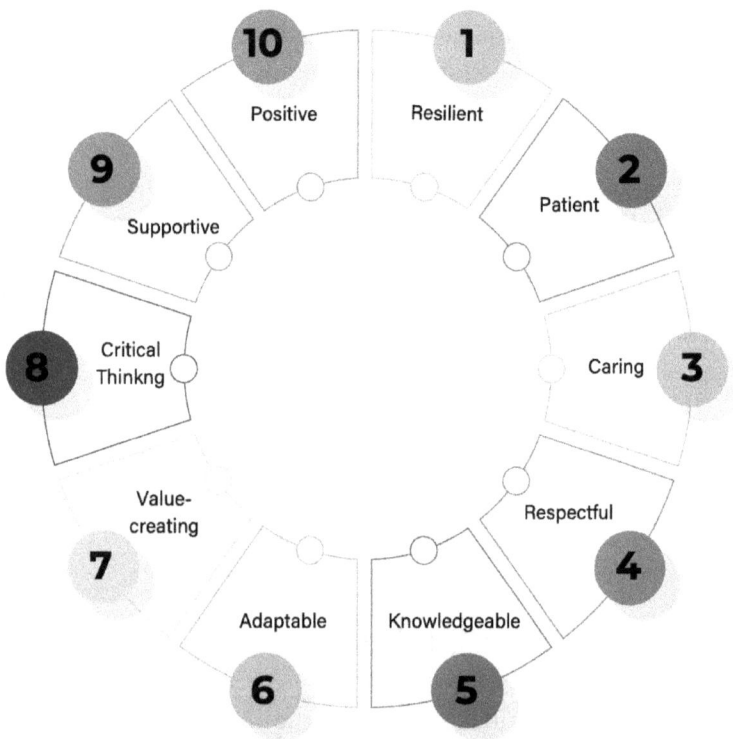

Figure 6. Circle of Ideal Qualities.

Once you have your list of desired qualities, compare that with what you and your kids know about their inner circle of friends. Then compare this with what you know about their online influences. Where there is a significant mismatch, you now have a solid foundation to have an intentional conversation about moving towards more value-creating friend relationships and online influences.

This also applies to other families. Who are the families you spend the most time with, and do your family values align? Are there families you should be spending more time with because of their positive influence on your kids and you? It can take some time, but you can certainly build your own community of families raising kids that create value in the world with a little effort. With the six communities of families I am part of, we meet once a month as a group to share practical family wisdom and continually build on it. These meetings typically last from ninety minutes to two hours.

If you search the internet for family leadership traits, you will find a lot. And yet, few families adopt, refine, and live what it means to be a leader within the family. Why is this? The same holds true for family budgeting. Every parent I meet says budgeting is something all families should do, but less than one in ten families consistently do it. Even most of those who say they follow a family budget admit that they could do this better.

If you don't really see the value in something, you won't do it. You can intellectually understand the value in doing something, but if you are comfortable enough without doing it, most people won't. Eating healthy and taking care of yourself is a great example of this. Most people know this is a good idea, but still have terrible diets anyway.

A couple of years ago, my older sister was complaining about stomach pain and generally not feeling well. I talked her into eating a clean diet. Within a week, she said she felt better than she could ever remember. Three weeks later, she was back on the old diet and feeling poorly again. I joked that she must be allergic to feeling good.

It is typical that most people won't consistently do what they know is good for them. There are many reasons for this, and I am not a psychologist, so I won't try to go there in this book. I will say that with the right family focus, it is easier to hold each family member accountable for doing what is best for them and the family. It's actually kind of cool having three or more loving accountability partners encouraging you.

Being a leader in the family means encouraging and nudging all family members to grow and create holistic value, individually and as a family. The primary job of a CEO is to continually and responsibly increase the value of their business. The same holds true for you as a leader in your family. Your job is to continually and responsibly grow the holistic value your family creates. The way you know you are moving in the right direction is to track progress on a family balance sheet that works for you.

As a leader in my family, I think about the family balance sheet in the three buckets of value creation I have been talking about in this book: material, emotional, and spiritual. I have already covered why each of these categories is so important and how each family and family member needs to find the right balance that works for them.

This doesn't have to be complicated. Material value creation is about objectively measuring whether or not your assets are growing. Emotional and spiritual value creation can be as simple as asking the question as a family once or twice a year, "Are we better, the same, or worse when it comes to creating value emotionally (what it feels like to be in the family) or spiritually (how connected we are as a family and to communities) than we were six months ago?" If the answer is yes, then we are moving in the right direction. There is power in having this conversation.

The way I set it up in my family and with the communities of families I work with is to see who is leading, participating, or not participating in creating value in each category. As a family, we look at progress in each category and ask what we can do to improve. Family members can take those ideas and be a leader in running with each of them. Other family members can participate in making those goals or activities happen. And some family members may choose not to participate at all.

I have worked with families where some of the kids initially wanted nothing to do with intentionally creating value within the family. I have seen it within my family. Typically, that changes within a year, and they start taking the lead in certain areas. It's hard not to get involved when everyone else is participating on some level. In the appendix, I give you some tools to create your family balance sheet and more. For now, here is some food for thought when creating your family balance sheet in each category.

MATERIAL VALUE (MONEY) FAMILY BALANCE SHEET

The material value creation bucket is perhaps the easiest to measure. Are your total family financial assets growing in value each year or not? If you grow your family assets by just 10 percent a year, they will double in just over seven years. It helps to set a goal and make it a family team sport to achieve it.

I started with nothing at seventeen, and forty-five years later, I have done really well financially. The first few years were touch-and-go, mainly living paycheck to paycheck. As I reflect, I spent the first twenty years building a foundation from which to grow my material wealth. From there, it really picked up speed. I like sharing this experience with those who say they have no money, so there is no hope for them to build financial wealth. Not true at all. This is another limiting belief example that is hurting many families.

I covered money skills in chapter 4 and how to apply them with a value-creation mindset. And there is a mountain of books and other resources on investing. I encourage you to do your own research on smart and responsible ways to build financial wealth. When I talk about wealth, I am talking about having a year or more of expenses in savings or other liquid assets. Having access to additional money in case of emergencies. Planning for and having enough income to live a comfortable lifestyle in retirement. More power to you if you want to grow your financial assets past that.

In the spirit of simplifying things, there are really only three ways to grow your financial assets. You can save it, loan it, or buy it. And there are safer, more responsible, and less risky ways to do each of these things. And of course, there are risky ways to play in each category. I prefer to be responsible and plan for the long run when it comes to growing my family's financial assets.

If you save one hundred dollars by putting it under your mattress for a year, and inflation is three percent that year, then your one hundred dollars will only have the buying power of ninety-seven dollars when you pull it out. If you put the same one hundred dollars in a savings account that pays two percent interest, you are better off, but your one hundred dollars is now worth ninety-nine dollars in purchasing power. Savings is a good way to have access to your money if you ever need it. The goal is to try to get an interest rate that exceeds the inflation rate, thereby preserving your purchasing power.

You can loan your money in a number of different ways. Loaning to friends can be dangerous, and it has almost never worked out well for me. You can loan it to the government through bonds, so they can build public works projects. This can generate interest income, usually tax-free or mostly tax-free. And the interest generated on average is typically higher than inflation when averaged over time. When the bond matures, you get all the principal back (the money you loaned). Just like savings, there are safer and riskier ways to loan money.

You can buy many different things that have a good chance of increasing in value over time. Buying a house can be one of these. Your home value can fluctuate from year to year, but since 1995, the median home value in the United States has more than tripled from $130,000 to $420,000. Of course, location matters a lot too.

You can buy ownership in public companies. Some of these companies pay dividends to shareholders. And over time, the stock markets have risen. Even after major crashes, the value is recovered, typically within a year. The same applies here; there are safer ways to buy stocks and some very risky ways. I highly recommend doing your own research when investing in stocks and requesting the assistance of a good financial advisor. Buying ownership in start-up companies can be one of the riskiest investments you can make.

If you are just getting started, you can keep a simple spreadsheet or ledger of all of your financial assets in these three categories. When you sum the three category totals, that number equals your family's total assets. You then take that number and subtract any debt you have. If you have $120,000 in total assets and you owe $20,000, then your total net worth is $100,000.

With this amount calculated, set a growth goal for the following year. If you want to grow your net worth by 10 percent, then your goal would be to have a net worth of $110,000 at the end of the following year. You will get better at this the more you do it. In the spirit of managing expectations, this could take up to twelve months to get in the groove, as long as you do the work, including educating yourself financially. Doing this work is a healthy and worthwhile struggle that I encourage you to undertake.

When I graduated from high school in 1980, I had about $6,000 in assets between my truck and music equipment. And I had $9,000 in debt that my parents charged up in my name. So my net worth was -$3,000. You really can start from anywhere and go everywhere if you put in the hard and smart work.

EMOTIONAL ENERGY VALUE FAMILY BALANCE SHEET

In chapter 2, I talk about positive emotional energy being the scarcest commodity in the world, in my opinion. It really does supercharge everything we do. For this part of your family balance sheet, it starts with awareness. What does it feel like emotionally when your family members interact with each other? I believe the goal for all of us is that family interactions feel great, and we look forward to being with each other. Even when times are tough, we choose family first.

Your emotional energy value family balance sheet is about tracking continuous improvement. Does it feel better today than it did six months ago? If the answer is yes, then you are moving in the right direction. And whether the answer is the same or even worse, you can always do things as a family to move more in a positive direction. Ask every family member to contribute their ideas to improve positive emotional energy within the family.

One idea a close friend of mine had for her family was to adopt the old adage, *If you don't have anything good to say, then don't say anything at all.* She was observing family members saying hurtful things, often disguised as joking, that were lowering positive emotional energy in the family. When her two teenagers and husband agreed to this new rule, it significantly changed, in a good way, what it felt like to interact within the family.

On your balance sheet, you are tracking progress over time. I recommend having this assessment conversation every six months or so. When you have these conversations, capture ideas to improve positive emotional energy from each family member. And follow up on previous ideas your family implemented to check in on how well they are working.

When creating value as a family, each family member has the opportunity to lead the effort, participate in the effort, or not participate at all. Ideally, we want all family members to take a leading role in creating value. And it is normal for kids, especially if you start this process when they are older, to take up to a year or two to get in the groove and participate.

Track the progress, ideas implemented to improve, how well they are working, and which family members are leading, participating, or opting out. As a leader in your family, you are nudging all family members to move in a positive direction. All kids seem to come with their own "built-in software" and go at their own pace and direction. The more loving and present we are on their developmental journey, the faster their progress will be.

Dual-household families can be more complicated to assess progress on improving positive emotional energy. I had a teenager in one of my communities recently say that when assessing positive emotional energy within her family, it was improving on one side of the family, and getting worse on the other side of the family. This was such a healthy conversation because the question brought out concepts that most kids won't usually talk about. And it helped her to see things in a productive and more emotionally evolved way.

SPIRITUAL VALUE FAMILY BALANCE SHEET

Evaluating spiritual value creation within a family is similar to evaluating emotional energy value creation. Is your family becoming more connected over time, and are you incorporating ideas to improve those connections? The spiritual value creation balance sheet will have a few more layers than emotional energy.

Connectedness is at the core of spiritual value creation, and it starts with each of your kids being connected to themselves. The goal is to help them better understand why they think and feel the way they do, and make decisions. This applies to all family members. From there, it goes to how connected your family is.

It's interesting to think back on my family members' connectedness when I was growing up. Everyone seemed to be in their own silo, with no intentional effort at all to strengthen connections between family members. This was not an ideal environment for me as a kid. And the life lessons from this experience have proven invaluable.

It takes just a little intentional and consistent effort to strengthen family connections over time. I see and feel the amazing progress with my sister and her grandkids from making this a priority. And I am seeing it across so many families in the communities I work with. This can be as simple as just having the conversation. "Does our family feel more connected today than it did six months ago?" And, "What activities and behaviors can we engage in that will strengthen our connection?" It's about awareness and prioritizing connections.

From family, it extends to communities. The best way to connect with communities important to you and your kids is to lean into them and add to the value they were formed to create. For your kids, it can be joining a sports team or a school band. And when they do, they work hard and help their group win and perform well. This extends to circles of friends and families. For parents, it can include any number of professional communities and nonprofits.

The magic from contributing value to various communities is that it will expose you to many more opportunities than you would otherwise have. This won't happen if you join a community and don't engage. You have to lean in and contribute to the value being created within each community. You get so much more by contributing first. Showing up within a community only to get something will not foster trust or add value to the community or your family.

Faith-based communities can be amazing for deepening your connection to a higher power and living a moral life. We need a lot more people leading in the world who are capable and, perhaps most importantly, moral.

Again, this can be as simple as having regular conversations that create awareness and foster ideas to strengthen the family. Every family is unique in how they want to create spiritual value.

Here is a starter list to consider when beginning these conversations:

- Your kids' understanding why they think and feel the way they do
- Your kids' decision-making process
- Strengthening connections within the family
- Choosing communities your kids engage with and creating value within them

- Choosing communities of families to engage with and add value to
- Choosing and engaging in business and philanthropic communities
- Choosing and engaging in spiritual and religious communities

You can find downloadable worksheets for Material, Emotional Energy, and Spiritual value Family Balance sheets online.

There are many moving parts within every family. At times, it can be overwhelming. As a leader within your family, you can simplify this by keeping everything in three buckets:

1. Going: Describing where your family is going when it comes to the value your family is collectively creating
2. Getting There: Having productive and loving conversations with all family members about how your family is going to get there
3. Getting Onboard: Highlighting what's in it for each family member to go on this journey

Imagine building your family's legacy significantly in your current generation. Then passing it on in a way that it keeps building generationally. I view inheritance when a family member passes as nothing more than *divide and hope for the best*. There is a reason why most family wealth is lost within three generations. When you are intentional about making it a team sport of growing your family's holistic balance sheet (material, emotional, spiritual), your family will develop and earn the capability to keep growing it generationally.

BIGGEST TAKEAWAYS FROM CHAPTER 7:

- How family members show up as leaders matters
- Every family member can be a leader
- Develop a description of what it means to be a leader within your family
- Engage in activities that create the most value for your family
- Be intentional about communities of families and circles of friends your family engages with
- Grow your family balance sheet: material (money), emotional (energy), spiritual (connectedness)
- Build on your family legacy generationally by making it a whole-family team sport

APPENDIX: GETTING STARTED

Creating a value-creation culture within your family will be easier than you think. It doesn't matter where you are starting from. Any place is a great place to start. You can apply what you have learned in this book at the pace that works for your family. The conversations around creating value are powerful in themselves for transforming your family's culture. From there, you can become increasingly intentional in how you apply these concepts within your family. There is no limit to how much value you can create as a family, but you have to start.

An easy way to get started is by joining our Dinner Table community. As of the writing of this book, we have tens of thousands of families in our Dinner Table communities and are climbing fast. We have monthly live calls covering many topics to help your family create more value. The practical wisdom shared between families in our communities is invaluable. We send out regular supportive content and have a community platform for our members to interact and access additional value-creation material.

You can start anywhere you choose, given what you've learned so far in this book and how you see it adding value to your family. Every family is unique, and the world is fortunate to have this diversity. I recommend starting with a monthly family meeting to discuss and refine family goals, everyone's job for the family (expectations), and what it means to be a leader in your family. Here is a simple example of what this can look like:

Barrett Family Goals:

- Have six months of total family expenses in savings
- Go on vacation to Alaska next summer
- Start an education savings account for each of our kids' college
- Have dinner as a family with no electronics, no less than 5 nights each week

Mom's job for the family

- Model being a leader in the family
- Model a healthy relationship
- Provide financial support to maintain the family's lifestyle
- Manage the family budget

Dad's job for the family

- Model being a leader in the family
- Model a healthy relationship
- Provide financial support to maintain the family's lifestyle
- Ensure all home maintenance is done consistently

Suzy's job for the family (8 years old)

- Keep your room clean and in order
- Do well in school
- Don't talk to strangers
- Care for your dog, Bandit

Austin's job for the family (17 years old)

- Drive and accompany your sister to events when Mom and Dad have to work
- Do well in school
- Grow your leadership capability within the family
- Build character traits, capabilities, and beliefs that will make you a successful adult

What it means to be a leader in the Barrett family

- Model healthy character traits
    - Integrity, grit, patience, empathy, self-reliance, and gratitude
- Promote structure and accountability
- Be a good problem-solver with a positive mindset
- Be a safe space to talk to
- Model healthy behavior
- Encourage the development of each family member
- Grow the family balance sheet:
    - Money (material value)
    - Emotional energy value
    - Spiritual value

It usually takes a couple of family meetings to have a solid list of family goals, everyone's job for the family, and what it means to be a leader. Next, I recommend adding goals for each family member. And I recommend building the list together during this monthly family meeting.

All monthly family meetings going forward will be discussing, refining, and checking in on your family goals, each family member's job for the family, family leadership, and each person's individual goals. My monthly family meetings usually take about an hour. Sometimes a bit longer, and sometimes less. And they are always energizing and fun.

When you are ready, I recommend monthly meetings with each of your kids to discuss their journey to becoming an adult. It will include developing and refining the character traits, capabilities, and beliefs that will enable them to be successful when they become adults. It also includes reviewing the three types of struggle and how they can leverage struggle to their advantage. This is a good time to refine their individual goals and capture their interests as well. Here is a simple example of what that can look like:

Showing up as an adult when Austin turns 18

- **Character Traits:**
    - Trustworthiness, patience, self-reliance, empathy, integrity, passion

- **Capabilities:**
    - Interview well for a job
    - Financial competency
        - Earn, protect, save, budget, spend, share, borrow, invest
    - Building a value-creation social circle:
        - Friends, mentors, groups
    - Communication skills (oral, written, persuasion)

- **Beliefs:**
    - I can be fully self-reliant financially
    - I can build financial wealth, so I can live a comfortable lifestyle in my later years without having to earn money from a job.

- I can live anywhere in the world I choose
- I can make a difference in other people's lives
- I can build momentum in my life, no matter what is happening around me

- **Struggles:**
  - Normal healthy struggles I am leveraging for my development:
    - Making the baseball team
    - Working through being nervous about speaking in front of groups
    - Getting better at time management
  - Unhealthy struggles and how I can use them to my advantage
    - Recovering and rehabbing from a broken arm in an accident
      - Learning patience, listening to my body, and learning how to better deal with pain. All of this will help me as an adult.
  - Intentionally designed struggles to build my ability to create value in the world
    - Starting and growing my own window cleaning business
    - Learning to play the drums and join a band by the time I am 18 years old
    - Start and grow a community youth group

- **Austin's individual goals:**
  - Get a new job in customer service to strengthen people and communication skills
  - Decide on an education path that will best support starting a business in animal support services

    - Earn enough money to upgrade the car next year
    - Go to South America with friends after graduating from high school

- **Austin's current interests:**
    - Wildlife and domestic animal protection
    - Solving problems
    - Exercise
    - Motorsports
    - Reading

These meetings, depending on the age of your kids, can last anywhere from ten minutes to an hour. I always facilitate these meetings with a mindset of seeing kids in my family as the potential they represent. I let them guide the conversation. I'm an encouraging coach.

To make it easy to manage weekly expectations and gigs for your kids, I recommend using a refrigerator printout like so many of our families do. This makes it easy to track your kids' weekly pay, where the money goes, expectations per their job for the family, expenses they are responsible for picking up, and action and brain gigs to earn money. See the following Figures 7 and 8 for examples of this; you can find downloads for your use online.

VALUE CREATION FAMILY

DINNER TABLE

Kid's Name:

Billy

Save	Spend	Share
30%	60%	10%

Max Weekly Pay: $35

Payday Date: Mar 5th

My Expected List
- [ ] Make your bed
- [ ] Clean your room
- [ ] Shower
- [ ] Brush your teeth
- [ ] Put away toys, books
- [ ] Clean your dishes
- [ ] Take out garbage
- [ ] Put away your clothes
- [ ] Clean bathroom
- [ ] Do homework

My Expense List
- Toys
- Video games
- Social outings
- Movies
- Special Events
- Extra clothes
- Trinkets/Souvenirs
- Birthday gifts for friends
- Gas (older)
- Car insurance (older)

Feb 27th - Mar 5th

Gig	Pay	Su 27	Mo 28	Tu 1	We 2	Th 3	Fr 4	Sa 5
Read nonfiction book - 20 minutes	$3.00/d	☐	☐	☐	☐	☐	☐	☐
Speak foreign language - 20 minutes	$3.00/d	☐	☐	☐	☐	☐	☐	☐
Sweep the floor	$3.00/d	☐	☐	☐	☐	☐	☐	☐
Vacuum the house	$3.00/d	☐	☐	☐	☐	☐	☐	☐
Organize the closet	$2.00/d	☐	☐	☐	☐	☐	☐	☐

Gig	Pay	
Wash & fold laundry	$2.00/w	☐ I Did It!
Wash & put away dishes	$4.00/w	☐ I Did It!
Make family dinner	$2.00/w	☐ I Did It!
Babysit siblings	$5.00/w	☐ I Did It!
Clean toilet and bathtub	$5.00/m	☐ I Did It!

Don't forget to mark off your Gigs in the Dinner Table app to earn your weekly paycheck

Dinner Table
© 2024 Dinner Table

Figure 7. Weekly Gigs Sample.

DINNER TABLE

Kid's Name:

_____

Save   Spend   Share
 %   %   %

Current Level   :_____
Max Weekly Pay :_____
Payday Date   :_____

My Expected List

My Expense List

_____
MM/DD - MM/DD

| | Su | Mo | Tu | We | Th | Fr | Sa |

Don't forget to mark off your Gigs in the Dinner Table app to earn your weekly paycheck

Dinner Table
© 2024 Dinner Table

Figure 8. Weekly Gigs Worksheet.

Make your family's dinner table discussions more value-creating. I practice having different family members lead dinner-table discussions around topics important to the family. These topics include upcoming vacations, checking in on goals, a family leadership topic, what the best part of each family member's day was, and more. Consider inviting guests over for dinner that your kids can learn from. Below, Figure 9 below gives you a simple way to plan for getting the most out of having these guests over for dinner.

The Dinner Table Plan

Who are the next 3 people we want to come to our dinner table this month?	What topic or purpose will we have for the dinner conversation?	What are the 2-3 questions you want them to talk to your kids about?

Figure 9. Dinner Table Topics.

Here are some questions to consider asking your dinner guests:

- What were the best lessons you learned as a teenager?
- What were your biggest turning points growing up?
- What values and beliefs were you raised with that helped you the most?
- If you were to talk to yourself as a kid, what would you say?
- Who were your mentors and what did they teach you?
- What advice do you have on relationships, money, and health?

- What was the hardest thing you ever accomplished and why?
- What's your biggest business success? Biggest failure? What did you learn from them?
- What were the best business lessons you learned?
- What are you most proud of in your life?
- How do you want to be remembered?

I really enjoy making family financial forecasting a team sport, starting with the family budget. Break out your family expenses in two categories, needs and wants, with the first line item being savings. And for each expense, assign a family member to own it. You can also have a separate budget for your kids. Not only can this be fun, but it also develops a valuable capability for your kids when on their own someday. See the following Figures 10 and 11 for examples. You can download copies for your use online.

VALUE CREATION FAMILY

MONTHLY HOUSEHOLD FORECAST

Monthly Income $ __5,353__   Month __November__

Necessary (Needs)   Plan   Reality   Sponsor

Category	Plan	Reality	Sponsor
Savings	$ 500	$ 400	Parent 2
Housing	$ 1,800	$ 1,800	Parent 1
Transportation	$ 800	$ 800	Parent 1
Food/Groceries	$ 700	$ 650	Kid 1
Communication	$ 262	$ 262	Kid 2
	$	$	
	$	$	
	$	$	

Sub Total $ 4,062 $ 3,912

Extras (Wants)

Category	Plan	Reality	Sponsor
Personal Care	$ 165	$ 205	Parent 2
Streaming	$ 50	$ 50	Kid 1
Meals out	$ 240	$ 375	Parent 2
Clothing	$ 300	$ 267	Parent 2
Pets	$ 175	$ 180	Kid 1
Entertainment	$ 300	$ 305	Kid 2
	$	$	
	$	$	
	$	$	

Sub Total $ 1,230 $ 1,382
TOTAL $ 5,292 $ 5,294
Difference between budget and actual +/- $ -2

TOTAL SAVINGS Balance $ 24,514

Dinner Table
© 2024 Dinner Table

Figure 10. Monthly Household Forecast.

MONTHLY KIDS FORECAST

Monthly income $ __320__   Month __November__

Necessary (Needs)   *Plan*   *Reality*   *Sponsor*

Item	Plan	Reality	Sponsor
Savings	$ 10	$ 5	Kid 1
School Supplies	$ 50	$ 20	Kid 1
Snacks	$ 10	$ 24	Kid 2
Clothing	$ 50	$ 45	Kid 1
Communication	$ 45	$ 45	Kid 2
	$	$	
	$	$	
	$	$	
Sub Total	$ 165	$ 139	

Extras (Wants)

Item	Plan	Reality	Sponsor
Toys	$ 20	$ 0	Kid 1
Hobbies	$ 10	$ 8	Kid 2
Entertainment	$ 50	$ 60	Kid 2
Treats + Sweets	$ 20	$ 15	Kid 1
Personal care	$ 10	$ 20	Kid 1
Pets	$ 20	$ 20	Kid 1
Gifts for friends	$ 20	$ 0	Kid 2
	$	$	
	$	$	
Sub Total	$ 150	$ 123	
TOTAL	$ 315	$ 262	

Difference between budget and actual +/- $ __+53__

TOTAL SAVINGS $ __112__

Dinner Table
© 2024 Dinner Table

Figure 11. Monthly Kids Forecast.

The goal of this book is to help you intentionally create value as a family, and get better at it every year. There is no end to how much holistic value you can create as a family. I encourage you to join our Dinner Table community by going to DinnerTable.com. This is a never-ending journey, and it is helpful and rewarding to be part of a community of like-minded families.

If you choose to join our Dinner Table community, you will receive the Value Creation Blueprint. It includes all of the key elements of this book in a format for you to build out your family's personalized value-creation playbook.

Here's to getting started!

BIBLIOGRAPHY

"Media Advisory: New Polling Data on Loneliness, Experts Available from American Psychiatric Association." American Psychiatric Association. February 26, 2025. https://www.psychiatry.org/news-room/news-releases/media-advisory-new-polling-data-on-loneliness-expe.

Deep-Dive Family Conversation Topics. Dinner Table Family, Inc. (2025). dinnertable.com. Retrieved from https://family.dinnertable.com.

Family Value Creation Goals. Dinner Table Family, Inc. (2025). dinnertable.com. Retrieved from https://family.dinnertable.com.

Monthly Household Forecast. Dinner Table Family, Inc. (2025). dinnertable.com. Retrieved from https://family.dinnertable.com.

Monthly Kids Forecast. Dinner Table Family, Inc. (2025). dinnertable.com. Retrieved from https://family.dinnertable.com.

The Dinner Table® Plan. Dinner Table Family, Inc. (2025). dinnertable.com. Retrieved from https://family.dinnertable.com.

Value Creation Blueprint. Dinner Table Family, Inc. (2025). dinnertable.com. Retrieved from https://family.dinnertable.com.

Weekly Expectations. Dinner Table Family, Inc. (2025). dinnertable.com. Retrieved from https://family.dinnertable.com.

Weekly Gigs. Dinner Table Family, Inc. (2025). dinnertable.com. Retrieved from https://family.dinnertable.com.

ACKNOWLEDGMENTS

To the teams at A for Arizona 1.0 and 2.0, and their work to improve K through 12 education in Arizona. This work opened my eyes to the challenge and root cause holding kids back from their true potential.

To Michael Rayball and Rebecca Chambers for their hard work and commitment to building a global community of families raising kids who will create value in the world.

To Rev. Janelle Wood and her Black Mothers Forum and School To Purpose Dinner Table communities. It's inspiring to experience the progress so many families are making as a result of their work and our monthly Dinner Table sessions.

To Monique, Jada, Aria, Alika, and Sabastian. Thank you for your commitment to creating value in our family.

To the team at Dinner Table. Thank you for leaning into our mission and pursuing our goal to positively impact millions of families.

To Mike Killion. Thank you for being such an amazing mentor and friend in my early business years. Your guidance helped solidify my approach to creating value.

To all those in the world creating positive value, and at the same time pushing back on anyone or anything intentionally taking value out of the world. You know who you are, and I applaud you.

ABOUT THE AUTHOR

Lee Benson is a seasoned business professional with over 30 years of expertise in value creation. He is the CEO of Execute to Win, which helps organizations of all sizes accelerate the value they create.

Lee's journey toward value creation began early when he used to pull weeds for 25 cents an hour at the age of six. Since then, he has founded eight companies, including Able Aerospace, which he grew from two to 500 employees and

2,000 customers in 60 countries. He is a renowned speaker and author on value creation, leadership, execution, and strategy. His work has been featured in various publications, such as *The Wall Street Journal*, *Forbes*, and *Inc.*, and by major media outlets, such as CNBC and Bloomberg.

Lee is also CEO of DinnerTable.com. Dinner Table® is a community of families raising kids that create value in the world, with over forty thousand parents in its community. Lee likes to say, "Kids today will be running the world of tomorrow, let's make it amazing!"

GIVE YOUR KIDS SKILLS THAT STICK FOR LIFE

dinnertable.com

DINNER TABLLE COMMUNITY

Dinner Table is a community that helps families raise confident, capable, value-driven kids. Join us and you will find support, engaging conversation, tools and resources that empower your family.

www.ingramcontent.com/pod-product-compliance
Lightning Source LLC
Chambersburg PA
CBHW071713020426
42333CB00017B/2244